SVERDLOVSK

F SOVIET SOCIALIS

D0548418

CASPIAN SEA

KI

AHLEVI

TEH

BAND

PERSIAN

ARABIA

NDIA

YEMEN

DEN

# *Lonek's Journey*

## The True Story of a
## Boy's Escape to Freedom

By

Dorit Bader Whiteman

Published in the United States of America by Star Bright Books, Inc.,
New York. The name Star Bright Books and the Star Bright Books logo
are registered trademarks of Star Bright Books, Inc.
Please visit www.starbrightbooks.com.

ISBN-13: 978-1-59572-021-4
ISBN-10: 1-59572-021-9

Printed in China 9 8 7 6 5 4 3 2 1

Library of Congress Cataloging-in-Publication Data

Whiteman, Dorit Bader.
  Lonek's journey : the true story of a boy's escape to freedom / By Dorit Bader
Whiteman.
    p. cm.
  ISBN 1-59572-021-9
  1. Lonek. 2. Jews--Poland--Jaroslaw--Biography--Juvenile literature. 3. Jewish children
in the Holocaust--Poland--Juvenile literature. 4. Holocaust, Jewish (1939-1945)--
Poland--Juvenile literature. 5. Refugees, Jewish--Soviet Union--Juvenile literature. 6.
Jews, Polish--Soviet Union--Juvenile literature. 7. Jaroslaw (Poland)--Juvenile literature.
I. Title.

DS135.P63L669 2005
940.53'18'092--dc22

2005010898

To Lily
For her cheerful interest,
her counsel and her affection.

# Acknowledgments

You might think that writing a book involves only one person: the writer. But that is not the case. A great many people are involved in giving birth to a book.

Probably the most important person is Lonek. This book is about him. I spent many hours listening to him tell me about his life. Then I wrote a book about his most unusual adventures and called it *Escape via Siberia*. The publisher of that book thought that the story of Lonek would make a wonderful book for children and suggested I contact Star Bright Books, a publishing company that creates beautiful and interesting books for children. The publisher of Star Bright Books agreed, and that made it possible for the book to reach you, the reader.

While I was writing this book, I thought it would be a good idea to check if young people really would find the story interesting. So I turned to Laura Conway, an English teacher at The Louis Armstrong Middle School in New York City. She gave a copy of the manuscript to each of the following children in her class: Alexandra Bahamon; Grace Bang; Samantha Barriento; Alexander Dediashvili; Karla Gomez; Jaimee Grant; Jacob Nieves; Alexander Pangourelias; Shamiur Rahman; Alif Alam, and Ryu Gregory. In addition, Jonathan and Louden Pluta, the nephews of my neighbor, also read the manuscript.

These children evaluated and commented on each chapter. Their enthusiastic, thoughtful feedback proved that the book would be interesting and exciting for children. Here are some of the children's comments: "A cliff hanger"; "There is so much suspense, I can't wait to read the next chapter"; "It keeps me on the edge of my seat"; "I don't want this book to end"; and "I need to know what happens next."

The children's comments also reflected the ability of *Lonek's Journey* to arouse deep feelings in readers, for instance: "It made me happy when Lonek was happy"; "I wept when the children were in trouble"; " I wanted to shout hooray when Lonek found his father"; "This chapter put a big smile on my face"; "A heart-wrenching but amazing story"; and "Wow, you blew me away!"

Feedback from the children also confirmed that the book would be thought-provoking and enlightening for children: "It gave me thoughts about what kind life I would have led if I had been born at that time"; "I want to know more about those places Lonek went to"; and "I thought a lot about the book's meaning."

And last but not least, the children helped me make sure that the book was written at a level that made for comfortable reading: "I understood everything"; "I think if anyone knows how to read, they would understand this book"; and "Everything was extremely clear."

Professionals, relatives, and friends all helped to create this book. My daughter Lily, who is a writer, helped by contributing excellent ideas. She took time from her own writing to lend her assistance and expertise. My husband Martin, who is very knowledgeable about history, offered useful suggestions, assisted in many practical ways, and was supportive at all times. He, as well as many friends, not only shared ideas with me, but was also

also very understanding. Whenever I was busy and could not participate in gatherings or other activities, they all sympathized and never became impatient. They always encouraged me to keep writing.

Of course, last but not least, a book needs to be read. And that is where you, the reader, comes in. Without you, the book would just stand on a shelf. But with you reading the book,the purpose of my writing is fulfilled. Thank you, reader.

On September 1, 1939, Germany invaded Poland from the west. On September 17, 1939, Russia invaded Poland from the east. Poland was then divided between the two countries.

*Aerial view of the center of Jaroslaw.*

12

# 1
# War

On a sunny day in August 1939, in his hometown of Jaroslaw, Poland, eleven-year-old Lonek was cheerfully walking home. He had been playing soccer with his friends and was now heading home to tell his father all about it. As he approached his home, he saw his father standing at the front door, dressed in the uniform of a Polish soldier. Lonek began to feel puzzled and frightened. In his small hometown, Lonek had rarely seen a soldier. His father was not a soldier, so why was he dressed like one? Lonek ran towards his father and asked him anxiously, "Papa, what is happening? Why are you dressed like that?" Lonek's father didn't smile the way he usually did when Lonek came home from school or was playing with a friend. Lonek's fear increased when his father answered him in a serious tone.

"Listen carefully, Lonek. I have to leave right away. The Germans are stationing their troops on our border and they might invade Poland. The German army is the strongest army in the world—it's much stronger than ours. But we must do everything we can to keep the Germans out of Poland. That is why all of our men are joining the army. While I am away, listen to Mama and do everything you can to help her. I will be back as soon as possible." Lonek's father quickly hugged him, picked up his bag, and walked off toward the center of the town.

All that summer, frightening rumors had been spreading through Jaroslaw. At first, the rumors had only been whispers, but by August they were no longer just rumors, but frightening possibilities. Lonek was aware that the adults around him were troubled and preoccupied. They spoke in low voices among themselves, so that the children wouldn't hear what they were saying. Lonek overheard words like "Hitler," "Germans," "Nazis," "invasion," and "war." Lonek, who was Jewish, knew that Adolf Hitler, the dictator of Germany, had contempt for the Poles, but Hitler had a particular hatred for Jews. He had heard that thousands of Jews in Germany had been arrested and imprisoned. The danger of Hitler ruling a country right next to his own worried Lonek at times. But most of the time he managed not to think about it.

For the most part, Lonek's life was happy. He liked his hometown. In contrast to many very poor towns Lonek had seen in Poland, Jaroslaw was pretty and had pleasant parks where he could play. He lived in a nice house with his father, mother, and three-year-old brother, Heimek. Lonek was eight years old when his father first brought Heimek home from the hospital. Back then, he wasn't sure if he wanted a little brother.

"Well Lonek, shall we keep him?" his father had asked.

Lonek took a long look at the tiny baby. Then he placed his little finger in Heimek's hand just as he had seen his father do. The baby curled his fingers around Lonek's. "Well, as long as he's here, let him stay," he replied. Now Lonek loved Heimek, who toddled after his big brother throughout the house.

Lonek was very proud of his father, who owned a broom factory that was just across the street from the soccer field. Lonek burst with happiness whenever his father came to watch him play soccer. Sometimes he came even if he had to leave work in the middle of the day. And his father was always doing helpful things for other people. For instance, he trained blind people in his factory so that they could earn a living. Many people came to Lonek's father for advice. Some of these people didn't know how to read and write, so Lonek's father wrote letters for them.

Lonek's mother owned a store in the town square where she sold the brooms his father produced. She also kept house and enjoyed playing with Lonek. The household included one other person whom Lonek loved: sixteen-year-old Sosa, his live-in babysitter. Sosa was a farm girl who took care of Lonek and Heimek while their mother worked. She took them to the park, where together they built beautiful sandcastles, and she was good at thinking up new and interesting games to play. Lonek thought of Sosa more as a playmate than a babysitter.

Lonek liked his neighbors. The ladies were like kind aunts who stopped to talk to him and frequently gave him treats. He liked playing with their children, too. On Jewish holidays, the families gathered around a big table, shared their food, and ate and drank together.

But Lonek also had problems, and school was one of them. It was not that he didn't like going to school. He did well in school and wanted to be as smart as his father, who spoke four languages. But some of Lonek's classmates hated Jews. Not just one or two of their classmates, but all Jews everywhere. They

15

teased and bullied the Jewish children at school. If any of the Jewish students did well on a test, they grabbed their test papers after class and ripped them up. In the playground, and after school, these boys and girls ran after the Jewish children and called them names. Since some of the teachers didn't like Jews either, they didn't protect the Jewish children.

Lonek often wondered why some people didn't like Jews. He asked his mother, who explained, "Unfortunately there are people who are so narrow-minded that they dislike anyone who is different from them in any way. They may not even know anything about Jews. They may not ever have even met a Jew. They are anti-Semitic."

As a result, Lonek did not mix much with the non-Jewish children, but he enjoyed spending time with his family, his neighbors, and their children.

A few days after Lonek's father left to join the army, Lonek suffered another loss. Late one morning, Sosa's father arrived unexpectedly with his horse and wagon. Because it took him many hours to travel from his farm to Jaroslaw, he usually stayed to talk and have a cup of tea with Lonek and his mother, but not this time. He quickly stated his purpose:

"Sosa must come home with me. I am worried about the Germans at the border. There is too much danger with Hitler threatening Poland. At a time like this, families must be together." He then turned to Sosa and said, "Come, Sosa, there is no time to lose." Sosa quickly gathered her belongings, and before Lonek could even get a goodbye hug, her father had pulled Sosa up onto the wagon and they had disappeared around the corner.

With both Sosa and his father gone, Lonek felt strange. He moped around the quiet house. Everybody seemed different. They were tense and irritable. People on the streets didn't smile or stop to say hello anymore. They hurried by; their minds were on other things. Housewives were busy buying food and storing water in case the Germans crossed the border into Poland. All the schools were closed. At any other time Lonek would have been happy if his school was closed for a few days, but this time it was scary. He wondered why the grownups thought it was too dangerous to keep the schools open. His only comfort was the thought that his father and the other Polish soldiers were ready to protect their country.

And then it happened . . . On September 1, 1939, the German army marched into Poland. The country was at war. For Lonek, the worst part was that he had no idea where his father was.

*A family fleeing from the German advance.*

# 2
# Surrender

As soon as the war started, many of the town's people loaded up their carts and wagons, piled as many family members as they could onto them, and fled. They headed east, away from Germany. Lonek's mother didn't leave. She was hoping that Lonek's father would come back. Some of their neighbors also stayed. Lonek heard them share the latest frightening reports with his mother:

"The German Air Force is bombing the whole countryside. Hundreds of villages have been destroyed," they reported. "The Nazis are rounding up people and taking them away," and "The Germans have faster planes and bigger tanks. We don't have enough planes. We can never win!" And finally: "The war is over. We have been defeated." It was all true. In only a few weeks, the Polish Army had been destroyed.

Lonek wandered aimlessly around the house as the hours dragged on. He thought about his father constantly. Where was he? Had he been killed? No! That was too dreadful for Lonek to even think about. Nor did Lonek want to ask his mother if she thought his father was all right. He knew that just asking the question would raise his mother's fears. What would they do without Papa?

Almost immediately after Lonek learned that the Germans had defeated the Poles, the sky over Jaroslaw darkened with German paratroopers dropping from the sky. Hundreds of armed men landed and set up camp in the town square. They marched around, bellowing commands and showing off their might to the local population. The women, children, and elderly people of Jaroslaw stayed inside their homes and closed their doors and shutters. Over the next few days, more German soldiers roared into town on motorcycles and in trucks. Worst of all, the SS appeared.

The SS was a military unit, specially chosen for its loyalty to Hitler. Clad in black uniforms with high leather boots and caps with a death's head emblem, they were a frightening sight. Lonek had heard that the SS was the Nazi party's most ruthless unit. It was made up of the cruelest men who had absolute power over everyone. They were known to be killers who showed no mercy, not even to children. They despised Polish people, but they hated Jews above all. Lonek's mother told him to stay inside and avoid the Germans at all cost.

About two weeks after the war started, Lonek's father walked in through the front door. Lonek was beside himself with happiness. His father was alive! His father looked exhausted and very worried. Lonek knew that his father's return meant that the Poles had truly lost the war. Now, no one was fighting for Poland. The country was at the mercy of the Germans.

"Papa, what happened?" Lonek asked.

"Loneki, it was terrible," he said. "The Germans have a powerful air force. They had many more planes than us. And their planes were faster and more powerful than ours. Many of our men were fighting on horseback against Germans tanks. The horses were terrified and bolted. The Germans also have more soldiers than us. We were helpless. Their tanks just rolled right over us."

On the day of Lonek's father's return, signs were posted throughout the town: all Polish soldiers had to report to the town square, where the Germans had set up their headquarters.

"Don't go," Lonek's mother begged her husband. "Don't report. Maybe they'll kill all the Polish soldiers! Why don't you run away?"

"I have no choice," his father replied. "If I don't report and they find me, they will shoot me."

Lonek saw that his father, who was usually so decisive, hesitated before he left for the German headquarters. Lonek ran after him and pleaded, "Papa, take me with you. I want to go with you."

"No, Lonek. You must stay with your mother . . . and stay away from the Germans." But Lonek would not turn back.

"Go home, Lonek!" his father insisted. Lonek kept following, and eventually his father stopped trying to make him go home. Without speaking they walked together toward the town square, which was usually filled with people. Now the square and the streets around it were deserted and silent. As they approached, Lonek saw a large table in the middle of the square where some seated soldiers were writing. A number of German officers wearing high black boots and thick leather belts were standing behind them. A line of defeated-looking Polish soldiers stood waiting to be questioned by a German soldier. Lonek and his father joined the line. The soldier in charge of the questioning looked hard and cruel. When it was Lonek's father's turn to report to the soldier, he stood at attention, saluted, and in response to the soldier's question, gave his name. At that moment, the standing officer turned to Lonek's father and roared:

"You Polish pig! Take off your hat when you speak to a German." And with that, the officer raised the whip he was holding and snapped it across Lonek's father's head. Lonek's father flinched and struggled for a moment to recover his balance. Lonek bit his lower lip back in order not to let a sound escape. Like his father, he stood motionless and stared straight ahead. His father's army cap fell off his head. Neither Lonek nor his father made a move to pick it up. Lonek knew that if they moved, if they uttered a single word, they might be shot. In his head, he could almost hear the sound of the German officer's gun firing. Those moments in front of the German soldiers felt like an eternity. And though he didn't know it yet, in that short span of time, Lonek's life was changed forever. A long journey was about to begin for him—a journey that would bring fear and hunger.

# 3
# Escape

As soon as the officer struck Lonek's father, two armed German soldiers stepped forward. They grabbed Lonek's father roughly by his arms and marched him away. Lonek's father was now a prisoner, and Lonek was terrified. He realized that the soldiers might kill his father. He followed them from a distance and saw them take his father to a large, fenced-in area near the train station. About a hundred Polish soldiers were already imprisoned there.

Lonek ran home as fast as he could. Gasping for breath, he told his mother what had happened. "Mama, they've locked Papa up! A soldier hit him with his whip. Papa was very smart not to answer back. They had guns and could have shot him if he had said anything. He was no more important to them than a fly!" Lonek sobbed.

Lonek's mother grabbed Heimek and the three of them hurried to the area near the railway station. When they finally saw Lonek's father behind the fence, they rushed over to him. They spent the rest of the day huddled on one side of the fence, with Lonek's father crouched on the other. They talked and cried together. Lonek saw many other Polish soldiers talking to weeping relatives through the fence. As darkness fell, Lonek's father told his family to go home. With the Germans in Jaroslaw, it was too dangerous to be out at night. So the three of them trudged home sadly.

Lonek couldn't sleep that night. At sunrise, he was dressed and ready to go. He packed some food for his father and walked toward the station. As he approached the fenced area where the Polish soldiers had been the day before, he stopped and stared. The whole area was empty. All the soldiers had disappeared. It took Lonek a moment to recover from the shock, and then he turned and ran home to tell his mother the terrible news.

With increasing terror, Lonek and his mother waited. They waited one day, then two, then three. But neither his father nor any of the other Polish soldiers returned to Jaroslaw. Although he didn't say so to his mother, Lonek was afraid his father might be dead.

On the fourth day, when Lonek and his mother were almost sick with worry, a horse-drawn, hay-filled wagon stopped in front of their house. The driver, a farmer dressed in dirty clothes and wearing a beaten-up old cap, dismounted and knocked on the door.

"I have a message for you," he said. He gave Lonek's mother a small, folded piece of paper. Without another word, he climbed back onto his seat in the wagon. Hunched over, and staring straight ahead, he sat and waited.

As his mother read the note, Lonek saw immense relief pass over her face. He knew instantly that the message was from his father. So that the driver couldn't read it, Lonek's father had written the note in Yiddish. It said, "Come immediately. Don't ask questions. Take whatever you can, and return with the driver." Between happy sobs, his mother exclaimed, "Your Papa is all right! We are going to him."

Lonek's mother grabbed a bed sheet and frantically began throwing clothes, bedding, and food into it. He saw her tuck some documents inside her blouse. Then Lonek watched in surprise as she picked up a hammer and smashed a hole in the bedroom wall. From there she removed a small metal box and opened it. Inside, there were a few gold chains and a gold watch, some jewelry, and some money. Lonek was amazed that his parents had hidden this box away, in case of emergency. Lonek carried his mother's bundle outside, and with the driver's help, hid it under the hay. He then climbed onto the wagon, and sat next to the driver. His mother followed, carrying Heimek.

"Mama, you left the door open," Lonek said, as he helped them onto the wagon. His mother looked straight ahead.

"Go!" she said to the driver.

Slowly the wagon pulled away from their house. Before long they were out of Jaroslaw. They knew that the countryside was filled with German soldiers and that danger was everywhere. No one spoke. The only sound was the clip-clop of the horses' feet. The driver stayed off the main roads, but in order to reach Lonek's father, the cart was forced to cross a bridge that served as a checkpoint for the German army. Heavily armed soldiers stopped and searched almost every passing vehicle. The driver turned to Lonek's mother and muttered in a raspy voice:

"If the soldiers talk to you, say nothing. Just shake your head 'yes' or 'no.' I will tell the Germans that you are my wife and

*German soldiers searching passing wagons.*

these are our children and that I am taking you home from a visit to your relatives." He turned his head so Lonek could hear what he was saying. "That way, the Germans won't suspect that your Papa was a Polish soldier."

As the cart neared the bridge, Lonek trembled with fear. He heard the rough voices of the soldiers shouting commands and insults at other travelers as they crossed the bridge. He saw a helmeted soldier point a rifle at a man and call him "a dirty Pole." As their cart passed the soldiers, Lonek kept his gaze fixed on the ground.

"Don't let the soldiers stop us. Don't let the soldiers stop us." He repeated to himself over and over again. "Don't let them kill us. I want to get to my Papa."

With some cursing and much shouting, the German soldiers

waved Lonek's cart on. During the rest of the trip, which lasted several hours, Lonek was so scared he hardly breathed. Each little sound and every shadow made his heart race. He thought he saw a scary, black-booted SS man behind every tree.

Finally the driver's farmhouse came into view. From a distance, Lonek saw a man standing in front of it, looking down the road as if he were expecting some one. Lonek assumed it was his father. Lonek jumped off the wagon to run toward him. But then he hesitated. His father had been neatly dressed in a Polish uniform when he saw him last. This man was wearing old, ill-fitting clothes. But yes, yes, it was his father! Lonek ran with Heimek toddling behind him. Lonek's father lifted him into the air and hugged him.

"Loneki! Loneki! I am so happy to see you."

"Papa, are you all right?"

"Yes, Loneki. I will tell you everything when we are alone."

The farmer and Lonek's father talked in low voices. They were making some sort of arrangement for the family to stay on the farm. Lonek watched as his father gave the farmer some of the money his mother had brought.

Lonek didn't like the look of the farm. The yard was poorly kept. The farmer's wife looked sloppy. She was carrying a crying baby and a little boy was running around the yard with a stick, trying to beat some squealing pigs. Lonek and his family followed the farmer into the house. It was dark inside, and it smelled terrible. The farmer's wife, who was not very friendly, gave them something to eat and then led them to one of the small rooms off the living room.

As soon as the family was alone, Lonek's father told them everything that had happened to him:

"All the men behind the fence in Jaroslaw were Polish soldiers. Fortunately, the Germans didn't know that I was Jewish, or they would have killed me. I didn't want to wait until they found out. I thought of the three of you—about how much I wanted to get back to you. I knew I mustn't give up hope, and that somehow I would manage to escape.

"At dawn, the Germans made us stand at attention. We were closely guarded by dozens of soldiers. Escape was impossible. We were marched to the train station. There we were herded onto cattle cars and the doors banged shut behind us. By chance, I was standing in front of a little opening and I could see the countryside passing by. I believed they were planning to kill all of us, so I said, 'We must jump off this train or sooner or later they will kill us.' The other men didn't want to jump—they thought we wouldn't survive. I tried to persuade them, but in life, we must each decide what is best for ourselves. I knew I had to try to escape.

"That night, as we were passing through a forest, I saw a curve coming up. As the train began to slow down, I pushed against the barred door, and to my amazement it opened fairly easily. I jumped off the train and ran into the woods.

"The German soldiers began firing—there were bullets whizzing past me. The Germans could not see me clearly because of the dark and the trees. They were just firing at random into the woods. Even after the train was gone I kept running. I was afraid some German soldiers might have jumped off the train and were chasing me. I ran and ran. I ran for my life. Finally, when I was completely out of breath, I threw myself on the ground and lay there until I was sure I hadn't been followed."

The sound of a branch snapping outside caused Lonek's father to stop and look up with alarm toward the window. He stood up, looked outside, and listened. When there wasn't another sound, he continued:

"When I got up, I realized my left leg was hurt. I knew I had to get rid of my Polish uniform because even if the Germans didn't find me, some Pole might betray me for the money he would get for reporting me. I saw laundry hanging on the clothesline of an empty-looking house. Stealing, I thought, is all right when it's to save your life. So I took a pair of pants and a shirt, put them on, and threw away my uniform.

"I knew I could not return to Jaroslaw because someone was sure to recognize me there and tell the Germans," Lonek's father went on. "So I took a chance and knocked on the door of this farmhouse. I knew it was dangerous because the farmer could have turned me in. I told the farmer that I was a Polish soldier hiding from the Germans. I figured he might be patriotic and want to help me. But I did not tell him that I was Jewish, because it was possible that he would report me to the Germans. Luckily, the German soldiers in Jaroslaw hadn't searched me, so I had some money. I gave the farmer what I had, and promised him more if he brought you here."

Lonek was impressed by his father's quick thinking and his bravery. It was good to know that his father was so resourceful. For the first time in weeks, Lonek began to feel safe. For a few days the family could rest at the farmhouse and decide what to do next. At least they were all together again. Lonek snuggled up in bed and fell asleep. But the night brought new dangers.

# 4

# A Second Try

The sound of the farmer and his wife quarreling woke Lonek in the middle of the night. He quickly but quietly woke his parents who listened intently to the furious words passing between the angry couple.

"Why did you bring those people here?" the farmer's wife hissed. "I don't want them in my house. It's dangerous having them here!" Lonek could not make out the husband's reply, but he clearly heard the wife say, "What if they are Jews? Then we'll really be in trouble. I want to go to the Germans and turn that family in." The couple then lowered their voices and Lonek could not catch what they were saying. But Lonek's parents had heard enough. It was clear they had to leave as soon as possible.

"Tomorrow morning, before the farmer's wife has time to go to the German police, I will offer the farmer money to take us to Sosa's father's farm. Her father is a wonderful man, and I think he might take us in." Lonek's father said.

Lonek was thrilled at the thought of seeing Sosa again—his babysitter, friend, and playmate. Early the next morning Lonek's father went to speak with the farmer who, for a hefty price, agreed to take the family to its new destination. Because of the great danger of being caught by German soldiers on the road, they had to wait until nightfall to leave. Lonek's stomach was in knots all that day. What if the farmer's wife managed to turn them over to the Germans?

Finally, it was night. The family climbed onto the farmer's wagon. The farmer was as relieved to get Lonek's family out of his house as the family was to be on its way. As the cart rolled slowly away from the farmhouse, Lonek wondered whether his life would ever be normal again.

The farmer kept off the main roads to avoid the German soldiers. He knew his own countryside better than the invading Germans, who were strangers to Poland. He figured that by taking back roads and by traveling at night they had a better chance of making their way to Sosa's farm undetected. Still, even at night, Lonek sometimes saw German vehicles searching for Poles and carting them off. In the forest he spied shadowy figures and heard voices in the distance. He didn't know whether they were Germans hunting Poles or Poles looking for revenge against the Germans. He assumed all those people had guns.

Lonek tried to ignore what he saw and heard. It was too scary. When he could, he slept on and off during the ride. Occasionally he heard Heimek crying as his mother tried to rock him to sleep. Lonek awoke as the cart reached Sosa's house. He could just make out someone running towards him. His heart leapt at the sight of Sosa's warm smile. The whole world might have changed, but Sosa was still Sosa. She threw her arms around Lonek and hugged him.

"Lonek, oh, Lonek I'm so happy to see you!" she exclaimed, "I've missed you. I've missed how we used to chase rabbits together. And our little sandbox! Do you remember the castles we built?" Lonek jumped up and down with excitement and happiness. He was so glad that she had not forgotten him. Sosa's father greeted the family warmly. He was grateful to Lonek's family for their generosity and kindness to Sosa during the six years that she had lived with them. But clearly he was worried. "We have to be very careful," he warned. "There are German soldiers everywhere. They check the farms. They check inside the houses. They check everywhere. We must hide you right away."

It was impossible for the family to live in Sosa's house. There were too many people coming to the house every day who might betray them to the Germans. Without wasting any time, the two fathers began digging out a space underneath the barn. They dug a hole just big enough for two adults and two children to sit in. They put wood planks along the sides so the hole wouldn't collapse. A trapdoor that could be reached by a small ladder covered the top. The top of the trapdoor was covered with hay so no one could see it. Their bathroom was a bucket.

Lonek stared at that little space with disbelieving eyes. This tiny area, a dark box that wasn't even big enough to lie down in, was now going to be his home. It smelled of the animals that lived in the barn above. But when Lonek thought of the black-booted SS men with their cruel eyes, he felt lucky just to have a place, any place, to hide.

Because the nights were getting very cold, Lonek slept in his clothes on a little pile of hay. Food was in short supply. If Sosa's family bought more food than usual, the neighbors might become suspicious that they were hiding Jews. Although they shared whatever they had, most days Sosa's family could only provide milk and cheese products which were made on the farm.

Lonek and his family never left their hiding place at night. During the day, they spent some time outside and in the farmhouse, ready to disappear into the secret hole at any moment. Once, while Lonek was in the house, a stranger walked in without knocking. Lonek raced to hide under a bed. He lay completely still, but his heart was beating so fast and so hard he was afraid the visitor could hear it too. He hid his face in his hands, as if his own blindness would prevent him from being seen. When he heard the footsteps go away and the door close, Lonek came out from his hiding place, but it took him a long time to recover.

Lonek was not only afraid for himself and his family, but for Sosa's family, too. He knew that the Nazis would kill the farmer, his wife, and even Sosa if they discovered that they were hiding Jews. He admired Sosa's family for being so loyal and so brave, and he felt grateful that they were risking their lives to help him and his family.

Lonek and Sosa's mothers soon became friends. Lonek's mother helped with the housework while keeping an eye out for anyone walking up to the house. When tradesmen came to the door, Sosa's father kept them out of the house by doing business with them in the yard. If a visitor insisted on coming in, Sosa's mother would step outside and claim that she was washing the floors and they were still wet.

*Germans and police about to search a home in Poland.*

Even though Lonek's family faced constant danger at the farm and had only a hole in the ground to call home, Lonek managed to keep his spirits up. His parents' presence reassured him and he trusted Sosa's father. And once in a while, he was even able to play with Heimek and Sosa in the yard. During those happy moments, Lonek managed to shut out the rest of the world.

Lonek and his family stayed with Sosa's family for about three months. But it became more and more difficult for Sosa's father to get enough food to feed both families. German soldiers came to the farm almost daily, and they took most of the milk and cheese Sosa's family produced. The tension of constantly having to be careful began to take its toll on both families. Finally, it was decided that Lonek and his family had to move.

"Where will we go, Papa?" Lonek asked.

"We will go east to the Russian side of Poland," Lonek's father said.

Lonek was confused. "Are we going to Russia, or are we staying in Poland?"

"Before Hitler invaded Poland," his father explained, "he knew that Stalin, the Russian dictator, would not like having German troops so close to Russia's border. He was afraid that Stalin might even fight the German army and throw it out of Poland. In order to avoid this possibility, and on the promise that Russia would not declare war on Germany, Hitler gave Russia the eastern part of Poland while he took the western part."

Lonek was amazed that a country could just be divided up this way, as if it were an apple. First Poland was Polish. Now it was half German, half Russian. "Is it better to be in the German or the Russian part?" Lonek asked his father.

"We don't know yet how the Russians will treat us," his father answered. "But I know one thing. The Russians can't be worse to the Jews than the Germans. No one could be, since the Germans are killing all the Polish Jews. I think we must try to get to the Russian side of Poland."

Lonek's father chose Lvov, a beautiful Polish city in the eastern part of Poland, as the family's destination. Once again, Lonek's mother wrapped the family's possessions into the sheet she had brought from Jaroslaw. Late at night, after a very sad goodbye to Sosa and Sosa's mother, Lonek's family climbed onto Sosa's father's cart and they started on the dangerous journey to the city of Lvov.

# 5

# Lvov

Lonek was very sad to leave Sosa, but he was also excited to be going into Russian territory. Lonek's parents told him about the beauty of Lvov, with its elegant buildings, green parks, and famous theaters. "It might be possible to lead a happy life there," he thought. "At least we won't be hiding from the Nazis."

Lonek knew what to expect of the journey when he climbed onto Sosa's father's wagon. Since the German army used the main roads constantly, they could only travel on back roads at night. In the darkness, the clopping of the horses' hoofs sounded so loud, Lonek feared they could be heard miles away. During the day, the family hid in the woods. They sat huddled on the ground, afraid that any noise would give them away.

At last, the family reached Lvov. At first, they were immensely relieved, but they didn't know where to go or what to do. Then Lonek's father had an idea. He asked Sosa's father to drop the family off at the main synagogue. Since that was where Jewish people went to pray, he guessed that many of the Jewish refugees might also go there to find their relatives and friends, and to get help. The family was lucky. A man at the synagogue told them that Lonek's uncle had already arrived in Lvov, and he gave them the address.

At first, Lonek's spirits soared when he saw the large, beautiful building in which his uncle was living. But he was shocked when he discovered that his family had to share a room with his uncle's family and more than sixty people. There were no beds. Everyone slept on the floor on straw mats, and there was no privacy at all. "Be happy you have a corner here," an elderly man said to Lonek one night. "Most refugees sleep in the streets."

"Yes," Lonek thought, "an overcrowded room was better than a hole under a stable." He was determined to make the best of life in Lvov, and he hoped that his father would eventually find them a better place to live.

Life in Lvov was much harder than Lonek had expected. It seemed to him that Joseph Stalin, the Russian dictator, was not much better than Hitler. Stalin looked down on all foreigners, particularly Poles, and passed laws that made their lives miser-

*The building in Lvov where Lonek and his family*
*shared a room with 60 other people.*

able. The NKVD, the Russian secret police, were everywhere, enforcing the harsh laws. If a Polish person did the slightest thing wrong, or often, even if they did nothing wrong, they could be arrested and disappear forever.

As the days passed, life became more difficult for Lonek and his family. Every day new homeless refugees arrived in Lvov. Finding food was an endless chore, and standing in line took up most of Lonek's day. The food shops and clothing stores had hardly anything to sell.

When the Russian soldiers first entered Lvov, they stormed the stores and bought or stole whatever goods they could lay their hands on. Almost overnight the stores were practically emptied. The Russians sent most of those items back to their families in Russia, where decent clothes, fine furniture, and choice foods had not been seen for years. They left almost nothing for the people who lived in Lvov.

In addition, the Polish people were afraid of being robbed. If they owned nice clothes or shoes they didn't wear them out on the street. They feared that a Russian soldier would stop them and demand they give up their coat or boots. No one dared say no—they knew the Russians had guns.

Once, Lonek saw a Russian soldier go into a store that still had sausages in stock. The soldier took all of them, wound the chain of sausages around his body, stuck a few in his boots, and cheerfully walked away without paying. There were none left for the people who had waited in line for hours. For every item needed, there was a different line. Sometimes Lonek would join a line even if he did not know what it was for. He knew that he would not get another chance to buy whatever it was the store was selling. Sometimes, after Lonek had stood in line for hours, the store owner would come outside and call, "Everyone leave! Everything is sold out!" There were many days when a little bread and some tea was all that Lonek was able to bring back to his family. And there were even days when he had to return home empty-handed.

Lonek was surprised at how neglected and rundown the city was. "Why is Lvov so dirty?" he asked his mother. "You and Papa said it was a beautiful place."

"For goodness sake, don't let anyone hear you criticize anything you see," she replied anxiously, "and especially never criticize the Russians—or Stalin! It's against the law. If anyone hears you saying these things, the Secret Police will arrest us. You can't imagine how sneaky they are. They always seem to know what people are saying." In a quieter voice she continued, "Before the Russians came, Lvov was a beautiful city. But Stalin hates all foreigners and the Poles in particular. Since Lvov is, or was, Polish, I suppose he doesn't care if it falls into ruin."

"Why can't people find a place to live? Why are there no apartments?" Lonek asked.

"When the Russians took over Lvov, they arrived not only with thousands of soldiers, but also with hundreds of government officials. They had to live somewhere. So they just threw the local people out of their homes and moved in themselves. On top of that, there are thousands of refugees like us. That is why there are so many people living on the streets."

Lonek could see for himself that the Russians had no desire

to take care of Lvov. The kind of services that most cities have did not exist in Lvov. No one collected the garbage. Lonek hated to see the dirty streets, the broken fences, and the ill-kept parks. There were plenty of Russian soldiers and everyone knew that the NKVD, the Russian secret service, roamed the streets, in and out of uniform. There were no regular police officers, and theft and violence were common. But it was impossible to complain without the risk of being arrested.

Lonek's parents had warned him never to talk about religion or to tell anyone that he was Jewish. The Russian government had outlawed all religions. It had closed the churches where the Christians prayed and the synagogues where the Jews prayed. Religious schools were also forbidden. No bibles, religious books or religious objects could be sold. Once Lonek saw a funeral procession where a cross had been placed on the coffin. The NKVD appeared, grabbed the cross, threw it on the ground, and chased the mourners away.

In spite of all these frightening circumstances, Lonek managed to adjust to his new surroundings. He was extremely relieved not to see German soldiers and Nazi officials around. He had a place to live. His father had found a part-time job, so the family had some money. Lonek enjoyed spending time on the balcony of his building, watching people pass by. Once in a while, his mother took him and Heimek to a nearby park.

One day, Lonek's parents asked him to go on an errand to the center of town, and to take little Heimek with him. The square was crowded and there were many small streets that led away from the center. Somewhere in the crowd of people, Lonek lost sight of Heimek. He was gone—he had totally disappeared! Lonek was desperate. He ran up and down the streets, shouting Heimek's name. There were many streets and Lonek couldn't find Heimek on any of them. In a panic, Lonek ran home. He was crying and shaking from head to toe. He told his parents what had happened. "It wasn't my fault! It wasn't my fault!" he sobbed over and over again. The fact that Heimek was lost sent his parents into despair. He had never seen his parents so frantic. His father, who had never hit him before, went into a rage and was about to strike him, when his mother cried out, "Don't! It's not Lonek's fault."

Lonek's parents were terrified because they knew that people disappeared daily in Lvov, and were usually never seen again. The brother of one man they shared their room with went to work one day and never came back. There was nowhere to go to for help. Once a person was lost, he was gone forever.

While the family was desperately trying to think of what to do, a scraping sound made everyone turn toward the door. The door opened. For a fraction of a second, no one moved. There in the entrance was Heimek! Little Heimek had found his way home by himself. The family rushed to him, and smothered him with hugs and kisses, asking over and over again, "How did you come back? How did you know where to go?" But Heimek just answered, "I don't know." Lonek and his parents laughed and cried with relief and happiness.

The incident brought home to Lonek's family how unpredictable life in Lvov was. Anything could happen. And it did.

# 6

# Footsteps on the Stairs

At four o'clock in the morning, most people are asleep. In countries run by dictators, it is the time that the secret police arrive.

One morning in June 1941, Lonek awoke to the sound of heavy boots stomping up the stairs. He heard a loud pounding on the door, and then a crashing sound as soldiers carrying rifles burst into the room. Lonek jumped to his feet. His first terrified thought was that the soldiers were Germans, and that the thing he feared most had happened: the German soldiers or the SS had caught up with him and his family. But while the soldiers were behaving very much like German soldiers, the orders they screamed were in Russian. He concluded that they were Russian soldiers. But it was clear to him that nothing good was in store for his family or any of the other refugees.

The people in the room scrambled up from their straw mats. Everyone was confused and terrified. No one could understand what was happening. The soldiers were shouting, waving their rifles, and smashing objects. They shoved and kicked anyone who was close enough. Children screamed in fear.

The Russians ordered all the men, old and young, and even the boys, to stand against the wall. Many of the soldiers looked

43

no older than teenagers, yet they were threatening men of Lonek's father's age. As the soldiers continued to bark their orders, Lonek's father helped an elderly man who had not been able to find his glasses make his way to the wall. Lonek followed his father, and stood next to him.

"Please, please, don't let the soldiers shoot us," Lonek said silently to himself. "We survived the Nazis. Don't let the Russians kill us now!"

While some of the soldiers held the men and boys at gunpoint, the rest stomped around the room screaming at the women to get ready. The women scurried around collecting anything that would be useful to take along, such as food or clothing. They searched and packed while their children cried in panic. Older girls tried to dress the young children who resisted because they wanted to be with their mothers.

After about ten minutes, the soldiers shouted, "Out! Everyone out, or we'll burn the place down!" The soldiers formed a human chain and relentlessly pushed the people toward the door and down the stairs. Although the women tried to help the old and sick, many of the elderly couldn't keep up. In the crush, some people fell, taking others down with them. But the soldiers never stopped shoving the people, many of them wearing nothing but their underwear.

"They are treating us worse than animals!" Lonek said.

"Quiet Lonek!" his mother warned. "They might hear you. Do you want to get us all killed?"

Lonek staggered down the stairs holding tightly onto Heimek, who was struggling to wriggle out of his grasp to get to their mother. Downstairs, open trucks were waiting. Lonek was fortunate to be loaded onto a truck together with the rest of his family. Many families were not so lucky. Lonek heard screaming and crying all around him, but he decided that that was really useless.

As soon as the truck was crammed full of people, it began to move. Lonek saw many other trucks that were full or being filled with people. As they drove through the streets of Lvov, he saw more and more trucks heading in the same direction. Lonek wondered where he and the others were being taken.

The trucks stopped at the railroad station. The station was filled with thousands of desperate people who, like Lonek and his family, had been rounded up in the middle of the night. Most of them were half-dressed, having grabbed whatever they could find when they were arrested. Everyone looked deathly afraid. Sobs and screams pierced the air. Tough-looking Russian soldiers were shoving the crowd toward the platform and onto a train that was so long, it was impossible to see its beginning or end.

The pushing crowd carried Lonek along. He was terrified that he would be separated from his parents. His mother clutched Heimek tightly in her arms. Lonek's father held on to the small bundle of possessions his mother had been able to rescue. He was pushing his way through the mob of people to help Lonek's mother climb onto the train. Lonek saw that many families had become separated. Parents were frantically looking for their children, and children were crying because they couldn't find their parents. Lonek held on to his mother's skirt with both hands, something he had not done since he was little. Over and over he said to himself, "I won't lose my parents. I won't lose my parents."

There were no steps to help the people get onto the train. Someone, who himself was being pushed, gave Lonek a shove up and he tumbled inside the car. Lonek was horrified by what he saw. He had traveled on trains before, but never on one like this. Those trains had seats and windows. This one had nothing but four, thick, solid walls. It was narrow, dark, and dirty. Lonek realized he was in a car that was normally used to carry cattle. He had seen trains like this when they passed through Jaroslaw, on the way to markets. Lonek wondered, "Do the Russians treat cattle as cruelly as they are treating us now? Is a Pole less valuable than a cow?"

Even though the car was already full, the Russian soldiers continued to shove men, women, children, and even babies into

*Russian soldiers loading people onto cattle cars for deportation to Siberia.*

it. Lonek guessed that there were at least fifty or sixty people already in the car. Surely they couldn't force more in! Lonek was squashed so closely to the others that he couldn't even look up.

Suddenly, they heard the clang of the sliding door being closed and bolted. There was a moment of horrified silence. Then some of the prisoners began to bang on the locked door. They begged to be let out, but there was no response. After a while, the protesting stopped, and an eerie silence settled over the car.

Lonek expected the train to start moving. But it didn't. It just sat there. As the hours passed, thin shafts of light crept in through cracks in the wall. Day began, but the train did not move. The air in the car got staler and hotter. The train just stood in the station. Lonek felt as though he couldn't breathe.

"If only the train would move," Lonek thought. "Maybe then there would be some air." But the train did not move. It stood in the burning sun for hours and hours. No one knew how long the unbearable waiting would last. Lonek heard Heimek crying and his own eyes filled with tears. Lonek wasn't sure he would survive this trip that had not even begun. He lost heart and felt despair.

Just then Lonek had an idea. Another boy was standing close to him and he realized that by both of them sitting down together and twisting their legs around each other, they could create enough space to sit. What a relief it was to finally rest his legs! From down low he spied a little hole in the wall of the cattle car. The opening gave Lonek a tiny glance of the outside world, and he felt that all was not lost. He remembered what his father had always told him, "Never give up hope."

"Papa is right," he thought. "We must never give up hope." Lonek promised himself that from that moment, no matter how bad things might be, he would always look for a small ray of hope. He decided that this was the only way to keep his spirits up and to carry on. With this determination, Lonek waited for the train to move.

# 7
# The Endless Journey

When at last the train pulled out of the station, Lonek was exhausted and tortured by thirst. Hour after hour the train rolled on. Lonek could tell by the change in the light that filtered into the car that he had been locked inside for more than twenty-four hours. At times he worried about where he was being taken and what was in store for him. But most of the time the suffocating heat and his agonizing thirst made it impossible to think about anything but relief. Just when Lonek thought he could bear no more, the train stopped and the soldiers slid open the barred door. Lonek thought that in his whole life the air had never smelled so fresh.

The women were given buckets and herded to the front of the train. Lonek guessed that the men had to stay back because the guards were afraid they might try to escape. Lonek's mother was gone a long time, and when she returned, her pail was filled with evil-smelling, oily water that had been drawn from the locomotive. The liquid was foul, but Lonek drank his share to the last drop. After a short time, everyone was herded back onto the train and the journey continued.

Once each day the train stopped and the prisoners were let out of the cars. They were given what could hardly be called a meal: a little weak tea or some watery, sour-tasting soup in which swam a small piece of moldy bread. The bread was smaller than Lonek's fist and so hard that Heimek couldn't eat it, even after his mother soaked it in the oily water. When his mother held him, Heimek put her finger in his mouth and sucked it as if it was a baby bottle. Lonek usually tried to break his chunk of bread into small pieces, so that he could make it last the whole day. Sometimes he saved a piece for the next day in case the train didn't stop, but he really wanted to swallow the bread in one bite to relieve his hunger for just a moment.

Lonek thought about his life in Jaroslaw. "Oh, to be back in my warm, comfortable bed now," he thought. He regretted the times he had protested his bedtime. He pictured the table in his old home set neatly for dinner. He remembered the delicious food his mother always prepared for the family. He thought about the times he had pushed his plate away, not wanting to eat. He promised himself that if he ever had another chance to eat his mother's cooking, he would always clean his plate and never be fussy again.

The worst aspect of the journey was the lack of clean drinking water. Lonek was constantly thirsty. He longed for rain when the water dripped through the cracks in the railcar. Sometimes the morning dew made the inside of the car damp. Then he would lick the moisture that collected on the nails in the walls. At some stations Lonek noticed wells for the local people, but the guards never permitted anyone from the train to go near them. The prisoners had to make do with the oily water from the locomotive. Lonek felt horribly embarrassed whenever he had to go to the bathroom. There were no toilets; there was only one bucket that stood in full view of everyone and was used by all the people on board. The odor was foul. The bucket could only be emptied when the train stopped.

During each stop, Lonek looked for his uncle's family, and for any of the people he knew from the building in Lvov. Although he searched for a familiar face, he never found one. The train was so long that it was impossible to see it from end to end and it carried thousands of people.

Lonek never wandered far from the car because he was terrified of the Russian guards. They didn't talk to the prisoners, only bellowed commands. "Back inside, you Polish pigs! Get on the train, if you don't want a bullet in your head!" they screamed when the prisoners had finished their pathetic meal. A few times, local citizens tried to bring food or fresh water to the prisoners, but the soldiers threatened to shoot if they came near. At almost every stop Lonek saw people who had died being removed from the train. Their bodies were left at the side of the tracks.

Lonek observed his father trying to keep the family's spirits up. He always remained calm and improved conditions for everyone in little ways. During stops, he searched the ground for pieces of metal or wood they could use for drinking cups. He also gathered leaves and branches and organized the families to take turns cleaning out the car when prisoners were allowed out for meals. Lonek was impressed by his father's thoughtful, practical, and dignified ways. His father's strength gave Lonek courage, but nothing could eliminate the torments of hunger, thirst, heat, sickness, lice, and fear of the unknown.

The train rumbled on and on for nearly three weeks. The prisoners continued to wonder where they were being taken. They guessed from the position of the sun that they were heading northeast. As the landscape became bleaker and bleaker, the surroundings more and more desolate, they began to fear the worst. Days and weeks passed in this journey of hell. Then suddenly, the train stopped in the barren wilderness and everyone was ordered off. Everyone wondered where they were. And then the dreaded word spread through the crowd—Siberia.

# 8
# Arrival in Nowhere

Lonek knew about Siberia. He remembered hearing grown-ups speak about it with a shudder. He had learned in school that Siberia was bigger than all of Europe. It consisted of more than five million square miles of plains, swamps, and dense forests. He remembered trying to imagine how big five million square miles was. He recalled with a shudder that parts of Siberia are so far north that in winter, the temperature can fall to sixty degrees below zero. Whenever Lonek had heard about prisoners sent to Siberia, he had pitied them. It had never occurred to him that one day he would be one of them.

Although the Siberian landscape looks desolate, deep in the ground lie valuable minerals such as coal and iron. The vast forests are a limitless source of lumber. But no one would choose to work in a place so cold, so unwelcoming, and so isolated.

The Russian dictator, Stalin, wanted the profits that could be obtained from these natural resources. For this, he needed a huge number of people to work in the mines and forests. He used the dreaded NKVD to arrest people on the slightest pretext, or on no pretext at all, and sent them to Siberia as slave laborers. Criticizing Stalin, or the Russian government, was enough of a crime for a person to be sent to Siberia. In addition, Stalin hated foreigners, and he believed that anyone who was not Russian was plotting against him and his state. So Stalin sent tens of thousands of foreigners living in Russia to the worst parts of Siberia, where they worked as slaves in gulags, or prison camps.

When Lonek and the others were released from the train, he gave a big sigh of relief. At least the terrible journey was over. But almost immediately, everyone was herded from the cattle cars onto trucks, which soon became as crowded as the cattle cars had been. They rode over dirt roads so bumpy that Lonek felt his last breath was being shaken out of him. When they finally stopped, the guards commanded, "Line up! March!"

Lonek and his family joined a line of people and trudged forward. Lonek stumbled on, falling from one foot to the other. He was tired, hungry, thirsty, plagued by flies and mosquitoes, and his head ached. The road led through swamps and dark woods. When the line came to a halt, Lonek saw in a haze of fatigue and sadness the final destination of their journey. He came face to face with the terrible reality. This was a gulag, a prison camp where people worked like slaves, until they died of cold, hunger, and disease. The gulag was surrounded by a wasteland of dangerous quicksand and dark forests. It was guarded on three sides by high towers. From up there, evil-looking soldiers armed with machine guns watched the inmates' every move. On the ground, guards with vicious dogs did the same. A river, too wide and rough to cross, ran along the fourth side of the camp. Escape was impossible.

A heavily-armed guard ordered the new arrivals to enter the camp. As Lonek's family and the other new arrivals marched through the camp, they passed a group of prisoners on the other side of a fence. A man called something in Russian. No one answered him. "Are you Polish?" he called out in Polish. Although no one was allowed to talk to the fenced-off Russian prisoners, Lonek's father walked to the fence and spoke to the man in a low voice. Lonek walked with him.

"How long have you been here?" Lonek's father asked.

Before answering, the prisoner chased away the woman standing next to him. "More than twenty years," the man said. "No one ever gets out. They will never let you go. You will die here. This is your last stop."

Lonek could not believe his ears. Was it possible that this terrible camp, this ugly, deserted place, was to be his home for the rest of his life? As Lonek and his father moved back to their group, Lonek asked, "Papa, why did the man make the woman next to him move away?" Lonek asked.

"That woman is his wife," his father replied sadly. "He is afraid that she will tell the Russian guards that her husband had criticized the government. For that, he would be severely punished."

Lonek couldn't understand why a husband would fear his own wife betraying him. His father explained, "These people have been in the gulag for many years. The guards reward any prisoner who spies on another prisoner. No one knows who's a spy and who's not. So now they no longer trust their friends or even their families." Lonek vowed never to allow this to happen to his family.

Lonek's gloom deepened when he saw the one-room shack

that was assigned to his family. It was tiny. It had a mud floor, and there were no windows. The walls were made of slats of wood that allowed in some light, and a little air, but also rain and snow. Lonek shuddered and wondered what they would do in the winter. There was no furniture, only a stove with one old, blackened pot sitting on it. He noticed that there was a hole in the ceiling over the stove, and assumed that it was for the cooking smoke to escape. The clay ceiling was pitted in places where big clumps had fallen off.

There were no beds in the shack. Lonek's heart sank when he realized the burlap bags on the floor stuffed with hay were where they would be sleeping. But he was so tired that even the sad-looking sleeping bags looked inviting. But how could he go to sleep now? It was still light outside.

"When will it be night, Papa?" he asked.

"It is night, Loneki," his father said gently. "We are so far north here that the sun hardly sets during the summer."

"I can't go to sleep," Lonek complained. "I am too thirsty and hungry. I want something to eat and drink."

His mother walked over to the stove, but she could not find anything to cook except some old, discolored potato peels. Lonek felt dismayed. He had hoped that once they arrived somewhere, the food would be better than the watery, tasteless soup they had been given on the train. The sight of the potato peels disgusted him. How could he eat those? It would not be long before he considered potato peels a luxury.

Lonek quickly learned that water was a luxury too. There was none in the house. His father knew that Lonek was too tired to go to the well for water. So he picked up the empty drum in front of the shack and went to get some for his family. This was a tiring chore that Lonek would later share with the other families living in that part of the camp. Where there is no water there can be no toilet. Lonek staggered to the foul-smelling outhouse and wondered how he would manage to reach it in winter when the snow would be far above his head.

When Lonek returned to the shack, he flopped down on his hay bundle wearing the only clothes he had. He closed his eyes and he heard Heimek crying. Lonek's head was spinning. Pictures of his journey tumbled through his mind: the night rides on the wagons, the terrible train ride, and finally the bumpy truck ride that had brought him to this horrible place. Above all, he saw the face of the prisoner who warned his father that they would never leave this place alive. Lonek had had nightmares before, but now he was living one.

Feeling despair creeping up, he looked for an idea to calm himself. He repeated to himself over and over again, "But we are here together. Mama, Papa, and Heimek. We are all here. We are all here." With those words, Lonek fell asleep.

# 9
# The First Day in the Gulag

Lonek awoke to shouting and a loud banging on the door. As he opened his eyes, he saw his father leave the shack. Lonek wondered where he was going. His mother was standing near the stove and Heimek was still asleep on the hay-filled bag. "What time is it? Where is Papa going?" Lonek asked sleepily.

"It's five o'clock in the morning," she whispered so as not to wake Heimek. "Papa has to go and work in the forest with the other men."

"What will he do in the forest?"

His mother sounded weary. "I don't know. We'll find out when he gets back tonight. When Heimek wakes up, we'll see if one of the neighbors can tell us where to get food."

By the time Heimek woke up, Lonek was so hungry that he would have been happy for a few spoons of the sour, watery soup they had been given on the train. When Lonek went outside with his mother and Heimek, he was struck by the emptiness and ugliness of his surroundings. All he could see were makeshift little shacks like their own, the elevated guard posts, and beyond them, dark woods. The paths near his hut were unpaved. Lonek pictured them turning to mud in the rain. They knocked on the door of one shack after another, but there was no answer. They realized that most of the occupants had been marched off to work. Finally, Lonek and his mother found a woman with a young child whom they plied with questions.

"Can you tell us where we can get some food?" Lonek's mother asked.

"Everyone gets a card which tells you exactly how much food you will get," the woman explained. "That is called a ration card. How much food you get depends on how much work you do. But you never get much. Mostly all you get is a little bread, a little flour and a few potatoes. If you don't finish your work, you get even less."

"But how do you survive on so little?" Lonek's mother asked.

"If you can find some berries and mushrooms in the forest, then you won't starve. But remember to put some food away for winter so you will survive when it gets cold." The woman paused as if to think of what other advice she could give the newcomers.

"You better look around and see if you can find some cloth to sew," she said. "The only clothes the Russians will give you are a parka, a hood and shoes with soles made from old cut up rubber tires. That's all." Then the woman looked at Lonek.

"How old are you?" she asked him.

"I'm eleven," he said.

"You're lucky. If you were a little older you would have to work like the rest of the children."

"Don't they go to school?" Lonek asked with surprise. The woman laughed as if he had made a foolish remark.

"School! Of course not! They work from five in the morning

59

until late at night. Your mama will have to work too, as soon as your little brother gets a bit older. The only reason she's allowed to stay home is because there's no one else to take care of your brother."

Lonek walked back to his shack with his mother and Heimek and waited uneasily for Lonek's father to return. He didn't come back until late in the evening. Because there were no chairs in the family's shack, Lonek's father dropped onto one of the straw-filled sacks. Lonek had never seen his father look so tired. In a low voice his father began to describe his day:

"We marched for many miles through the woods until we came to a clearing. The Russians gave us saws and axes and told us that we each had to cut down twenty-two trees. The amount of work you are assigned is called your quota. Twenty-two huge trees! We are not allowed to talk or to sit down. The soldiers watched us every minute. After just a few trees, I was so tired; I thought I couldn't go on. But the soldiers told us that unless we achieved our quota our food rations would be taken away. I thought, if I don't make my quota we will get less food. If I get less food, I will have even less strength to cut down trees. And then I thought of all of you, and I knew I had to keep going until I had cut down all twenty-two trees.

"You know, most of the men have never done this kind of work before," he continued. "We aren't used to such hard physical labor. It was exhausting. I know the older men won't be able to keep up, and when they don't, they will starve. I heard one of the men complain to the Commandant, the head of the camp, about the harsh conditions. The Commandant replied, 'You will get used to them or you will die'."

Lonek was shocked at such cruelty. "A woman told us that children work here too. What do they do?" Lonek asked.

Lonek's father looked down at the floor as if he did not want to tell Lonek the truth. He realized, however, there was no point in keeping it from him. Lonek would find out soon enough.

*Child in a Russian gulag.*

"Well, the children, the children!" Lonek's father exclaimed. "It's terrible how they treat the children! They are given big saws to cut the branches off fallen trees. They are very heavy but the children have to carry them to the sawmill. Sometimes, when big trunks are sent across the river, the children have to stand on them to direct them to the other side. The trunks keep turning over in the water, and the children have to keep running to keep their balance. Most of the children are soaking wet all day long."

"What if a child falls into the water? Don't the tree trunks roll over them?" Lonek's father did not answer. He just looked away.

Knowing that she would eventually be forced to work, Lonek's mother asked, "What do the women do?"

"Well, they carry heavy logs, dig ditches, and shovel manure," his father answered hesitatingly. "I have heard that some are sent to work in mines, but fortunately, there are no mines around here."

After Lonek's father stopped speaking, the family sat silently on the floor. No one could think of anything to say. Just then, Heimek toddled over to Lonek and dropped some stones that he had collected that day into Lonek's hand. He looked up proudly and laughed a small child's laugh. The family looked at Heimek and at each other. They knew that for him, if for no other reason, they had no choice but to carry on.

# 10
# Survival in the Gulag

Lonek's family knew that they had to focus on one main goal—survival. Every single day was a struggle. They also tried to maintain some pride and dignity.

Lonek's father began by making their shack a little more livable. In the brief moments when he was not working, he built shelves and a table and a bench from wood Lonek found in the forest. Now the family no longer had to keep their food on the floor, where it was difficult to keep away the insects and mice.

Lonek's father also made them a wooden tub. The water had to be hauled from the communal well, and even though it was always cold, Lonek enjoyed taking baths in the warm weather. He felt wonderful when he splashed in the water.

It was essential to try to stay clean to avoid the many diseases that thrived in the Siberian gulag. Diseases that were considered minor illnesses in Jaroslaw, were major in the gulag. Scratches and cuts easily became infected. Typhus, scurvy, dysentery, and pellagra were common in the gulag because of the filth and lack of decent food. And mosquitoes from the marshes brought malaria.

Despite the many diseases that plagued the prisoners in the gulag, there was no medical care. Although the camp had a hospital, it was too far away for a sick person to reach by foot, and there was no other way to get there. Lonek had heard his mother talk about a woman who asked the camp Commandant if she could use one of the workhorses to carry her sick daughter to the hospital. He refused, saying the horse was needed for more important matters. The woman carried her child all the way to the hospital in a snowstorm. When she finally got there, she was told there was no room. They were not even allowed to stay for a few hours until the snowstorm passed. The mother then carried her child through the storm all the way back to their shack.

Even if a prisoner managed to reach the hospital, they received little or no care. The hospital was dirty and had almost no medicine or equipment. There were no beds or blankets. Sick people simply lay on the dirty floor. Lonek knew he had to stay well.

Lonek's mother did her best to care for her family. Because none of them had a change of clothes she constantly repaired the clothes they wore. She traded berries and mushrooms for scraps of cloth, and because Lonek and Heimek were growing, she patched their threadbare pants and shirts into larger sizes.

She also tried to keep up Lonek's schooling the best she could. She taught him whatever she could remember from her own school days. She managed to borrow a book from one of the other prisoners to help Lonek improve his reading. She also told him stories about their family and about Poland's past, so that Lonek would have a sense of history.

But Lonek's mother's main worry was to obtain enough food to keep her family alive. The food ration that Lonek's father earned when he fulfilled his work quota was not enough. The small portions of bread, flour, and mealy potatoes left the family constantly hungry.

Lonek was always looking for ways to help his family. In fact, he became an essential provider of food for the family. He learned from some Russian prisoners who had lived in the gulag for years where to search for red currants, berries, and mushrooms in the forest. They also told him how to spot the poisonous mushrooms that could be deadly.

In summer and fall, Lonek roamed the woods alone, searching for food. It was not an easy task. He constantly battled bouts of fear. He worried about picking poisonous mushrooms by mistake. He was also afraid of bears, wolves, and other animals that lived in the forest. The howling wild animals frightened him. At times he was not sure whether the howling he heard came from an animal or the wind. And there were mosquitoes everywhere.

Lonek was also terrified of getting lost. The forest was dark, and most of the trees looked alike. He tried to use oddly shaped trees as landmarks to help him find his way home, but several times he did get lost, and he felt so frightened that he could not think. But then he would make himself sit down on a tree stump and remember his mother's words:

"If you fear that you are lost, sit down, calm yourself and think. If you panic you can't think. Look for the sun. It sets in the west. If you know which way is west you can figure out which direction to go."

Lonek also managed to catch fish. Because it was forbidden to go near the river, he always went at dawn to avoid the prison guards. He fished with a metal basket hanging from a string that his father had made for him. He waited patiently without moving until a fish swam into the basket and then yanked the basket up by the string.

Lonek's mother always gave him a big welcome when he returned from his food-finding trips. She praised him for his courage and admired the berries or fish as she cleaned them. Whenever they could spare some, she carefully tied the mushrooms on a string to dry them for winter. The terrible, sunless, freezing winter arrived early. The snowfall was endless and deep. Soon the snow was piled so high that the door of the family's shack could not be opened. Lonek's father dug a tunnel so that they could get in and out. No matter what the weather was like, his father had to go to work. Neither snow nor illness was ever an excuse for not working.

Once the rivers froze it became more difficult for Lonek to fish. But his family needed the food he brought even more desperately in winter, when there were no berries or mushrooms. Using a small piece of wood or metal, he spent hours scraping a hole through the ice on the river to reach the water below. As Lonek worked, his fingers grew numb and his toes froze.

"It's so cold that when I spit it turns to ice in midair," Lonek told his mother when he returned. "Even if I don't go far, I get so cold I feel as stiff as a piece of wood by the time I come home."

Despite the severe discomforts, Lonek never hesitated to go out looking for food. He knew how important his help was to his family and he was extremely grateful that he still had all his family. He knew many children in Siberia who had no one. Some of them had been separated from their parents before they arrived in Siberia. Others had lost their parents to disease or starvation in the gulag. Lonek admired the many resourceful things these children did to survive.

One little girl told Lonek that she fetched soup from the kitchen for adults who were too tired at night to go and get their own portions. For each bowl that she brought, they gave her a spoonful of soup. Another girl went from shack to shack and sang little songs. Sometimes an adult would reward her with a little piece of bread or some soup. A fourteen-year-old boy who worked all day in the forest mended shoes at night to earn extra food to try and keep his sick parents alive.

Some of the things Lonck saw and heard made him extremely sad. Once, he saw a small child gathering and eating grass because she was starving. A boy who worked in the flour mill confided to Lonek that at times he was so hungry that he would grab a handful of flour and swallow it quickly before the guard noticed. Another boy confessed to Lonek that he felt ashamed because he had to beg for food. Lonek told him not to be ashamed, because all the prisoners were doing what they had to do to survive.

Seeing so many orphans made Lonek worry about his own parents. He was mostly worried about his father's health. He didn't know how they would manage if his father became ill. Fortunately, Lonek's father had been given a new job. Instead of cutting trees he now worked with metals. He no longer had to walk as many miles back and forth from work. But he still had to do twelve hours of hard labor every day. In winter, he often arrived home with frozen hands and feet. In summer, mosquito bites covered his face, arms and legs.

Anyone who missed work or arrived late was jailed for days or months in a rat-infested prison. This meant that their families lost precious food rations. The men who ran the camp had no pity for any of the people in the gulag.

"Those who don't work have no right to live," the Commandant said.

Lonek was very angry with the Russians for treating the Poles and the Jews so harshly. After all, the Jews and Poles hated the Nazis as much as the Russians did and would have liked to fight the Germans.

Lonek tried his best not to show it, but sometimes he truly felt despair. "Papa, do you think we will ever get out of here?" Lonek sadly asked his father one day.

"Yes I do, Lonek," he replied.

"But don't you remember the man who told us on our first day that we will never leave here? I think he was right. Stalin will never let us go! He wants us to slave away as long as we live."

His father put his arms around him and said, "Don't despair, Loneki. As long as we are alive, there is always hope."

"Nobody knows we are here. Nobody cares. No one will ever rescue us." Lonek began to cry.

But Lonek was wrong. The rest of the world had not forgotten the prisoners. A miracle was about to occur.

# 11
# Behind the Scene

Lonek and his family slaved in the Siberian gulag through the bitterly cold winter. By the summer of 1942, they had been in the prison camp for an agonizing year.

Outside the gulag, the world had changed in important and unexpected ways. But the prisoners were unaware of the changes. The Commandant of the camp did not allow the guards to speak to the prisoners. Newspapers were not allowed inside the camp. The prisoners did not know the course World War II was taking.

Events were taking place that were to have an enormous impact on the prisoners. In 1939, Hitler had signed a pact with Stalin. At the time, Hitler had agreed not to invade Russia if Stalin allowed the Germans to take control of the western part of Poland. But that was only a pretense on Hitler's part. His real plan was to conquer Russia. In June 1941, Hitler broke the pact and ordered the German army, which was the biggest and strongest in the world, to invade Russia.

It was well known that Stalin, the Russian dictator, trusted no one. He suspected almost everyone of having plans to betray him and to undermine his power. So it was odd that he believed Hitler when he promised not to attack Russia. Stalin was completely surprised and unprepared when thousands of German soldiers marched into Russia. The German army was the strongest in the world. They had fierce tanks that rolled over everything and everyone, and a large air force that dropped bombs mercilessly on both soldiers and civilians. Stalin realized that Hitler's war machine was so strong that Russia could not survive the German attack unaided. So Stalin sought help from England, which had already been at war with Germany for two years.

England agreed to help Russia, but demanded that Stalin release the thousands of Poles who had been imprisoned in jails and gulags. Of those who were released, 70,000 former Polish soldiers and 30,000 civilians were allowed to join the British army. Stalin was a tyrant who never let anyone out of his clutches, but he knew that without help from Britain, Hitler would conquer Russia. Stalin made his decision, and to everyone's surprise, he agreed to Britain's demands. He promised to provide food and uniforms for the Polish army and to provide a Polish general to lead the troops out of Russia.

But where could a Polish general be found in Russia? General Wladislaw Anders, a famous Polish general, had been been captured and imprisoned by the Russians when they invaded Poland in 1939 and was at that time in Russia's worst prison. On August 12, 1941, General Anders was freed from the fearsome Lubianka prison in Moscow to guide 100,000 Poles out of Russia.

Among those who would follow him out was Lonek.

*General Wladislaw Anders (far right) with his troops.*

# 12
# The Gates Open

Although Stalin had agreed to free the Polish prisoners from the gulags in Siberia, the prisoners themselves had no idea that they were free. No one told them. The Commandant of Lonek's camp kept the news secret because he wanted to hold on to his slaves. Who but slaves could be made to cut down twenty-two big trees every day, and do heavy labor in the blazing sun and freezing cold?

The Commandant's secret was discovered when a package wrapped in an old newspaper arrived for the Commandant at the gulag. A prisoner working at the Commandant's house, eager for any news from the outside world, straightened out the crumpled newspaper, and read with amazement the report that Stalin had agreed to free the Polish prisoners.

It took a few seconds for the news to sink in. But when it did, the man let out a yell that echoed throughout the gulag. He began running in circles, waving the newspaper above his head. He laughed and cried for joy, and in his excitement shouted words no one could understand. Afraid that the commotion would bring the guards, some onlookers tried to calm him down. But he continued to laugh and babble uncontrollably. Finally, they became impatient with him. "What in the world has happened? What is the matter with you? Calm down and talk. The guards will come!"

After awhile, the man began to pull himself together. "Look! Look at this newspaper! It says here that we are free! We can leave!" He shouted. "The Germans have invaded Russia. There is a war on. Now we can fight the Germans!"

A man grabbed the newspaper and began to read it aloud. When he finished, the people began to cheer, to weep, to throw their arms around each other. And then they ran to tell the others. The word "freedom" spread from mouth to mouth and in an instant the whole gulag was in an uproar. The prisoners ignored the furious guards who ordered them to return to work. No longer slaves, the prisoners paid no attention to them. Instead the now free men, women, and children ran to their shacks to gather their few possessions.

The Commandant pleaded with the former prisoners to remain in the gulag. He promised to give them better food and housing and easier working conditions. The prisoners laughed in his face. The Commandant could do nothing but follow the instructions he had been sent. He was forced to give each prisoner some food, a small amount of money, a ration card, and to let them go. With not much more than the clothes on their backs, the prisoners walked out of the prison.

Lonek was beside himself with joy. He could not believe what was happening. A few days earlier he had almost given up hope, and now his family was really, really leaving! His whole family was alive and they were leaving this horrible place together! He could not stop jumping and laughing. He had not laughed so hard even once during the many months since he had left Jaroslaw.

His father, resourceful as always, quickly transformed the family's wooden table into a wheelbarrow. In it went their few possessions: the little bit of food they had, the clothes his mother had stitched together from rags, Lonek's fishing tool, and the few toys his father had made for Heimek.

As Lonek's family hurried toward the entrance to the camp, Lonek noticed the Russian prisoner who had warned Lonek's father that they would never leave the gulag alive. The man was still trapped behind the fence. Lonek knew that he and the other Russian prisoners must be envious, and disappointed that they could not leave the gulag along with the freed Polish prisoners. He felt sorry for the man, and he waved goodbye to him. Then, pushing the wheelbarrow in front of them, Lonek and his family left the camp without a backward glance.

The former Polish prisoners had only one question on their minds: how to join General Anders and follow him out of Russia. They had read in the crumpled newspaper that General Anders was assembling his army in Tashkent. The problem was that Tashkent was in the south of Russia while Siberia was thousands of miles away in the north. They had been transported to Siberia against their will. But no one lifted a finger to help them go south. They had to find their own way to Tashkent. All they had was a little money and a small amount of food, as well as the ration card they had been given when they left the gulag. It was not much, certainly not enough for a journey that would take at least a month, and maybe even longer.

Some of the prisoners managed to reach one of the big Russian rivers and boarded a ship that carried them to the south. Others tried to hitch rides on carts, hoping to get more rides along the way. Some, in their desperation to get as far away from the gulag as possible, started to walk, hoping they would find a better solution in time.

Lonek's family decided to try to find the railroad tracks and to follow them to the nearest train station. There they hoped to catch a train that would take them to Tashkent. They walked for two days and nights on muddy roads for seemingly endless miles. The walk was long and difficult, but Lonek skipped happily ahead of his family. Now that he was free, nothing could discourage him.

*Poles, freed from the gulags, en route south to join General Anders' Army. This is the kind of truck Lonek traveled on.*

The family finally reached the train station. Lonek was shocked to discover that thousands of other released prisoners had reached it before them. People were living on the station platform while they waited for a train. No one had enough money to rent a room and everyone was afraid to leave the station because they didn't know when a train might arrive. Lonek and his family joined them.

Day after day, Lonek waited for the train to come. He had heard that trains were scarce because they were needed to carry Russian soldiers to the battlefields to fight the Germans. There was no way of knowing when the next train might come. Lonek found a lookout position at one end of the platform. He watched and waited for nearly two weeks without any sign of a train. Each day the train station became dirtier and more crowded Finally, Lonek heard the chug-chugging of an approaching train.

"It's here!" Lonek shouted to his father. "Get ready! Hurry!" He knew there wasn't much time. As the train pulled into the station, hundreds of people on the platform pressed toward the stopping train. There was no order, no lines. There was only chaos created by desperate people.

"We can't let anything stop us now. We must get on this train," he repeated to himself. He knew that this might be the last train that would ever pass through the station. Lonek didn't care whether he found a seat or not. He was willing to crouch on the floor in some dark passage. With a great deal of pushing and being pushed, Lonek's family managed to get aboard. Within a few minutes the train began to pull out of the station. Lonek managed to reach a window and looked out as the train moved.

He knew how lucky he was when he saw that hundreds of stranded people remained on the platform.

Lonek soon realized that this journey was going to be just as difficult as his previous ones. The train moved at a snail's pace and made frequent unplanned stops, some of which lasted for a day or more. The crammed cars overflowed with people. The train became dirtier and dirtier. The passengers were hungry and thirsty. At each stop, people poured out of the train and into the surrounding fields in search of something—anything to eat. Lonek saw people eat grass and weeds, just to get the feeling of having a full stomach. Because Lonek was good at finding food, he got off the train at each stop and looked for something for his family to eat.

During these stops, Lonek never knew when the train would start up again and was always terrified of being left behind. But Lonek was lucky. He always managed to get back to the train in time. He had seen some people left in the fields as the train pulled away.

He saw two brothers get separated. At each stop, the older brother would get off the train to search for food. The younger brother stayed on board, worrying frantically that the train would leave before his brother got back. He had already lost his parents; his brother was the only family he had. He clung to his brother's jacket and begged him not to leave. But the older boy insisted that if he did not search for food, they would both starve.

At one of the stops, the train took off before the older brother managed to get back. The younger brother was in despair. He sobbed and cried uncontrollably and hid his head in his hands. He called his brother's name out loud. The other passengers were unable to console him. Suddenly, by a lucky twist of fate, the train stopped. The older brother was able to catch up and jump aboard.

The travelers faced other dangers, too. Occasionally, thieves boarded the train and robbed the passengers of the few possessions they still had left. Even more frightening was the appearance at various stops of the secret police who attempted to arrest some of the travelers and return them to the gulags.

Although Lonek often felt frightened, nothing could dampen his spirits. He sat in his little corner and day-dreamed about Tashkent—a mysterious, ancient city with a reputation for beauty. He pictured his father going to work so that the family could live in a comfortable apartment while waiting to follow General Anders out of Russia. He dreamed of his family once again sitting around a table talking and eating his mother's delicious cooking. He was sure that Tashkent had parks, and that his mother would take him to them as she had done in Jaroslaw. He imagined running and playing as he used to, with Heimek running happily after him. He thought that surely, this train was taking him to paradise.

After about five weeks, Lonek and his family arrived in Tashkent. What he found was quite different from what he had imagined.

# 13
# Tashkent

What made Lonek's life so different from a normal life was its unpredictability. Lonek felt as if he were riding a giant roller coaster. He never knew whether he was about to head up or down, whether the next moment would bring relief or more misery. When Lonek's family moved to Lvov he had hoped that their lives would improve. Instead, they were deported to Siberia. Then, when Lonek believed that he would be trapped in the gulag forever, its gates suddenly opened and his family was free. Tashkent proved to be just as unpredictable.

Lonek had heard that the city was a wondrously beautiful place. He had high hopes that his life would now be better. But when Lonek and his family finally arrived in Tashkent, what they found was a dirty, poverty-stricken city that was overrun with refugees. Among them were thousands of Poles who, like Lonek, had made their way to Tashkent in the hope of joining General Anders. There were also thousands of Russians in Tashkent who had fled from the advancing Germans.

Tashkent was filled with homeless people who lived and died on the streets. The constant starvation left the refugees with little resistance against illness, and most of them looked desperately sick. People could not wash themselves or their clothes. They infected and re-infected each other constantly with various diseases. Lonek often saw children nursing sick parents on the street. Many went begging so they could buy a little food to help keep their parents alive. But most passers-by had nothing to spare, not even a penny. When Lonek saw a crying child sitting near a man or woman, he knew that child was about to become an orphan.

Lonek and his family were among those lucky enough to have a room. Most refugees who managed to find a place to live lived in cellars, barns, stables, shacks, or mud huts. His father had found a tiny room, just big enough for the four of them to squeeze into at night to sleep. Food was always difficult—sometimes impossible—to obtain. Lonek had to stand in long lines, just as he had done in Lvov. Frequently there was no food in the stores. When there was, the local citizens would often push the refugees out of the line and prevent them from buying anything.

One day, Lonek noticed a small potato field not far from where they lived. He was sure it was strictly forbidden to go there. The next morning Lonek got up before dawn and went there while it was still dark, but it was too late. He discovered that the field had already been harvested. As Lonek's heart raced from the fear of being discovered he found a few tiny potatoes that had been overlooked by the farmer. He dug out the potatoes with his bare hands. But a few potatoes remained buried too deep for him to reach. He searched for a small branch and dug up the hidden treasure. Lonek also went to a nearby stream where he sometimes managed to catch fish. Since he didn't have a line or net, he constructed a small waterfall with rocks from the bank of the river. He caught the fish as they went over his waterfall.

Most days Lonek came home with something to help feed his family. Sometimes it was a few potatoes, sometimes it was a fish, and sometimes it was nuts or fruit gathered secretly from a farmer's tree. No matter what he brought home, his mother was good at making some edible dish out of it. She made soup out of nuts, and used the potato peels to stretch the little food they had.

"Lonek, you are so smart," his mother often said. "Whenever you go out, you always come back with something. You are such a big help."

In spite of Lonek's efforts, the family was sometimes reduced to eating grass bricks meant for feeding camels. When raw, they were poisonous for humans to eat, but when cooked they became edible. Although they tasted awful, the family at least felt that they had something in their stomach.

Lonek and the other Polish refugees had heard that the English government and private organizations were trying to help them. They knew that these organizations had sent food, medicine, and other supplies. But cargo ships carrying supplies were constantly being bombed or hitting mines, and frequently never reached Russia. And when they did, there was a shortage of trucks to get the crates to where they were needed. Almost all the trucks in Russia were being used in the war against the Germans. As a result, supplies had to be transported by donkeys and camels—the slowest possible means of getting help to where it was urgently needed.

In addition, Stalin's distrust of foreigners interfered with getting the supplies to the refugees. Even though the English were fighting on Stalin's side, he did not trust that they were really aiding in the formation of the Polish army but suspected them of spying on the Russians. As a result, he blocked Britain's effort to help the Poles, and supplies rarely reached the refugees. Amidst all this misery, there was one wonderful little ray of happiness for Lonek. He found a friend. It had been a long time since Lonek had had a friend to play and laugh with. Life in Lvov and the gulag had been too difficult to think about playful things. But in spite of Lonek's fight for survival in Tashkent, a friendship began between him and a Muslim boy.

The boy was from Tashkent and lived a normal life; he went to school and had a proper home. At first, the two of them played and laughed together without being able to communicate. Slowly Lonek learned a little of the local language, Uzbek, and his new friend taught him more. He took Lonek to his school and introduced him to his friends. Lonek had not been in such a normal setting in a long time. He had not been inside a school since his own school was closed just before the Germans invaded Poland. He could hardly believe that there were still children in the world who got up in the morning, washed, ate breakfast, went to school, spent their day in class and returned with homework in the afternoon. That kind of life seemed like a dream. When he lived in Jaroslaw, he never imagined that he would miss doing homework. Now, he would have given anything to lead such a normal life.

Lonek's friend even invited him to his home. Lonek entered

shyly and greeted his friend's parents, who talked to him kindly. On one of his visits, his friend's parents gave him some food to take back to his family. He ran home and excitedly said to his mother, "Mama, do you know what I saw? You'll never believe it. It was amazing!"

"What is it, Loneki? You look so excited," she said.

"Mama, I saw a kind of trunk. It was made of straw and is round on top with a beautiful design. It was big—really big. And when it was opened, I saw it was—Mama, you won't believe it— it was full of pita bread! I didn't know there was so much bread in the world. It was better than seeing a trunk filled with gold. Look what they gave me!" And with that, Lonek pulled out four pieces of bread and gave one to each member of the family. To them, the bread really was more precious than gold.

Despite occasional moments of happiness, the family's situation did not improve. Lonek's father got sick—too sick to do the kind of physically demanding jobs that refugees found, such as carrying heavy sacks of flour or moving bricks. Now, there was no money. In addition, Heimek was suffering from painful toothaches. Without money they couldn't afford a doctor, dentist, or medicine.

Lonek's mother realized that the family's survival depended on her. It was clear to her that she needed to buy nourishing food that might renew Lonek's father's and Heimek's strength, but she wondered how she could earn enough money. She came up with the idea of trading some of the fish or nuts that Lonek brought home for cloth, and selling the cloth on the street. Each sale would only bring a few coins, but that was better than nothing. Lonek was troubled by his mother's plan. He knew that it was illegal to sell anything on the street. If she were caught, she could be sent back to a gulag. But Lonek's mother knew that she had no choice. She had to take the risk. To Lonek's list of daily worries he now added the fear that his mother might be arrested and disappear like so many other refugees.

Every morning Lonek's mother took the fabric she was going to sell and hid it under her clothes. With the money she made from the first sale, she paid a man to take her across the river on a raft. She decided she was less likely to be recognized or arrested on the other side of the river, since no one knew her there. Sometimes she only sold small pieces of cloth for very little money, but it was better than no money at all.

One evening, Lonek's mother came home exhausted and shaken. Lonek could hardly believe her story. "I was crossing the river on the raft I usually take," she told him. "Suddenly, the raft turned over and was swept away. I fell into the river. The fabric got wet and became so heavy I didn't know whether I could swim across. I thought I would drown. The raft's owner just swam away and didn't bother to help me. Somehow I managed to reach the other side of the river and crawled ashore. I was so exhausted. I just lay there and could not move."

"What did you do, Mama? Why didn't you come right home?" Lonek asked.

"Oh, Loneki. I couldn't waste the day or the fabric. I unrolled it and laid it out on the ground to dry in the sun. Then I went to the square and sold it for as much money as I could get," she said. "I had to sell it for less because it was so crumpled."

Lonek was in awe of his mother. He felt she must be made of steel. It was comforting to know that she would go to any length to help her family. But he worried about her.

At one point, his mother managed to obtain a large piece of soap which she decided to sell in the streets. Soap was a most desirable item. Few people had any. But even fewer could spare money for such a luxury. To hide the fact that she was selling the soap, she asked Lonek to stand on a side street holding the bulk of it. She cut off two or three small pieces at a time and returned for a few more after she sold them. Every time his mother disappeared around the corner, Lonek's terror began to rise. He was sure that the NKVD would discover what they were doing and take them both away.

It was summer, and the heat in Tashkent was unbearable. The combination of the blazing sun and Lonek's fear made him feel even hotter. The hours seem to drag by endlessly. He felt dizzy and weak. His stomach was contracting from tension and hunger. Occasionally his mother bought a little drink for him made from pickle juice. It was the cheapest drink you could buy. It tasted sour, but at least it was cool. Every time his mother came to get another piece of soap, Lonek would plead, "Mama, let's go home! Please Mama, I want to go home."

Many nights Lonek went to sleep hungry. He drank water just to fill his stomach. As he lay in bed, he kept wondering, "How can I get just one little piece of bread?" The fear that he may not have anything to eat the following day haunted him in his sleep. But it was no use complaining. He knew that his father was helpless and his mother was doing all she could do for them.

And even though he tried hard, he could not gather enough fish or potatoes to keep the family alive.

In spite of all Lonek's mother's efforts to nurse and feed his father, he lay helpless on the slab of wood that served as his bed and he became sicker and sicker. He was feverish and perspired continually. He needed medical attention, but even if the family had been able to find a doctor, they couldn't afford to pay him. A nurse finally visited and gave his father two pills. They didn't help and she never came back. Lonek's mother didn't know what was wrong with Lonek's father. She searched for some medicine but could find none. The only thing she could do for him was to dip a cloth into cold water and place it on his burning forehead.

Heimek also began to suffer from frequent infections. His hearing became affected. His teeth began to rot and had to be pulled out. Lonek's mother was terrified that Lonek would get sick, too. And so she made a desperate decision. Of all the terrible experiences that Lonek had lived through, his mother's decision was the most heart-breaking.

# 14
# Abandoned

The road seemed endless. Lonek and his mother had started walking early in the morning. Now it was getting dark, and they were still walking . . . walking . . .walking. The countryside was dusty and dry—almost desert-like. At one point they crossed a riverbed that had been dried out by the hot sun. Only a trickle of murky water remained. They were alone. Just once every few hours would they pass someone else along the road. Lonek cried almost the whole time. Occasionally, his mother cried too. But they kept on walking.

"Mama, please don't do this!" Lonek sobbed. "Why do you want to get rid of me?"

"Loneki, how can you think I want to get rid of you? I don't want to get rid of you! I want to save your life. Your papa is sick. Heimek is sick. I don't have enough food to feed you. You are going to get sick and die."

"But why are you only sending me away and not Heimek?"

"Heimek is still a baby. There is no one to take care of him but me. I wish I could find a better place for him, too."

"When we were in Siberia, Mama, it was so cold. I could have died there from the cold. But here at least it's warm and I won't freeze to death. I even have a friend here, Mama."

"It's the food, Lonek. We have no food."

"But Mama, haven't I always found food? I will find more food. Do you remember the berries and mushrooms I picked? And the fish I brought? You always said I was such a big help!"

"Listen, Loneki, you've always helped the family as much as you could. Without you, things would have been much worse. But now that Papa is sick, he can't work anymore. You can't keep us all alive by yourself. I'm your mother. I don't want you to leave, but I have to try and save you."

They walked in silence until Lonek asked, "Why are you taking me to an orphanage, Mama? I'm not an orphan!"

"I know, Lonek. I just hope they will take you anyway."

Lonek had heard about the orphanages. He knew that thousands of Polish children, whose parents had died or disappeared, were wandering around Russia. Because they were in constant danger of starvation and were being hunted by the NKVD, Polish officials collected as many of these children as they could find, and placed them in orphanages. There, the children were looked after and were safe from the NKVD while waiting to join General Anders.

The orphanages were not comfortable places. They were very short of food and clothing and were filled with diseases. But they offered some food and a roof over the children's heads, and that was more than most children, including Lonek, had.

Eventually Lonek stopped pleading with his mother. He knew that he could not change her mind. He continued to sob quietly and once in a while he was aware that his mother was crying, too. Lonek had no idea how far they had walked, but by

*Two hungry orphans.*

the time they reached the orphanage it was dark outside. His mother rang the bell. A man opened the front door. His mother explained to him that she wanted Lonek to be taken in by the orphanage.

"I'm sorry, we don't have any room left," the man said wearily. "We have no place to put another child. As it is, the children are already sleeping in the hallways."

"I don't care what you have," his mother answered firmly. "Lonek has to stay. I'm not taking him back."

Lonek was shocked by the tone of his mother's voice, and by her words.

"I'm sorry. There's no room here," the man said and closed the door.

Lonek's mother bent down, kissed Lonek, and said, "Don't

worry. They will take you." And with that, she turned around and walked away.

"Mama, Mama! Don't leave me here!" Lonek called.

But his mother was gone. She had disappeared into the darkness. Lonek was alone.

For a while Lonek just stood in front of the door without moving. He was in shock. He didn't know what to do. He felt totally abandoned. After some time he sat down on a low, stone wall and waited. His hand touched a piece of fruit that was growing near him. Because it was round he thought it was an apple. But when he picked it he realized it was too soft. He bit into it. It tasted odd and slightly sour. He didn't realize that it was a tomato, because he had not seen one in years. For some reason, the strangeness of the fruit made him feel even more alone.

Hours passed. Lonek just sat on the wall in a fog. If he tried to walk home he might get lost, or the NKVD might pick him up. So he sat there. Suddenly the door to the orphanage opened and the man he had seen before stepped out. "Come in," he said.

Lonek followed him inside mechanically. The hallways were filled with sleeping children. Without a word the man pointed to a narrow space between two children already asleep on the floor. Lonek lay down. He was so exhausted that he fell asleep immediately.

What Lonek didn't know at the time was that his mother hadn't left. She had been hiding, but had continued to watch Lonek until she was sure that he was safe inside the orphanage. Then she started off in the dark on the long walk home.

# 15
# Among Strangers

Lonek was woken up by someone shaking him by the shoulder. A strange man was leaning over him. "Hurry. Get up. We are leaving," he said. Lonek looked around in confusion. Where was he? Who were all these people? Why were they in a hurry? Where were they going?

There was no need for Lonek to dress. He was already wearing all the clothes he owned. Someone handed him some tea in a small, broken cup and a small piece of bread. Several young men who were dressed in a combination of old Polish army uniforms and tattered clothes were helping the children. Lonek guessed that they were counselors, and, by their dress, that they had been in the Polish army. The counselors directed the children to form a line and began moving them out to waiting buses. Lonek heard the name Anders over and over, and concluded that the group was leaving to follow General Anders' Army. He noticed that most of the orphans had nothing but the clothes on their backs.

Suddenly, a terrible thought hit Lonek. He was about to lose his parents! He wouldn't be able to write to them because their hastily built shack had no official address. And he certainly had no address for wherever he was going. A horrible fear gripped Lonek. His family would never be able to find him! Lonek felt great sympathy for the orphaned children he had seen in Siberia and in Tashkent. They were always searching for their parents. Now he was about to become an orphan himself.

Lonek's bus took them to a train station. There, everyone boarded an old, shabby passenger train. Once again, the memory of the horrible cattle car that had taken him to Siberia came flooding back. But at least this was an ordinary train with seats and windows.

Few of the children spoke to each other. To Lonek, most of them seemed absorbed in their own thoughts and memories. Lonek assumed that they were thinking of their parents, sisters and brothers who had either died or been left behind somewhere. Maybe, like Lonek, they were wondering what lay ahead.

Lonek sat huddled in a corner seat by a window. He spoke to no one and no one spoke to him. Silent and suspicious, he wondered about the counselors. Who were they? Where were they taking him? Could they be trusted? They had been soldiers in an army. True, they had been in the Polish army, not the German or Russian army. But still, after the many terrible experiences Lonek had had, could he trust any soldier? Perhaps these men had bad intentions that would only emerge later.

As the train moved out of the station, one of the counselors handed each child a little box that looked like a tin of sardines. Lonek inspected his box, and then carefully and slowly rolled back its lid. What a surprise! Instead of containing real sardines, the box contained pieces of deep, dark, delicious-looking chocolate in the shape of sardines. Lonek had not seen a piece of chocolate since he left Jaroslaw. He licked a chocolate sardine hesitatingly. Yes, it was chocolate! Sweet, delicious chocolate! Lonek had almost forgotten that chocolate existed.

The men must have put a lot of effort into finding such a rare treat for the children. Perhaps these men weren't bad people after all, Lonek thought. And perhaps they were taking him to a better place where he would get food and clothes. A tiny flame of hope lit up in Lonek's heart.

The chocolate had a relaxing effect on the children. They began talking, and the conversation quickly turned to the one topic they had in common: how they had come to accompany General Anders' army.

"My parents and sister died in the gulag and I was left all alone," began a girl who looked slightly older than Lonek. "I sold my boots and tied some rags around my feet. That's how I walked through the snow. With the money from the boots I was able to travel for a while. When the money ran out I nearly starved to death. Luckily, a Polish soldier saw me and he took me to an orphanage. And now I am here."

Lonek was surprised to hear that the girl had come willingly to the orphanage. But he was even more surprised to learn that some of the children pretended to have lost their parents in order to increase their chances of being accepted by the orphanage. He listened to a girl who was about his own age tell her story:

"I had heard that children in the orphanages had food. So, with my two sisters and my brother I stood in front of the orphanage for many days. They didn't believe that we were orphans. They gave us some food so we would tell them where our parents were. But we kept saying that they had died—that we didn't have a father or mother. After a while they took us in. We didn't say goodbye to our parents, and we have never seen them again." Lonek thought how hard it must have been for these children to leave without saying goodbye. He also became aware that other families had to make choices like his mother made for him—whether to leave or stay with a sick parent.

A boy related, "My father was very sick. I would have starved to death if I had stayed with him so I came to the orphanage. Every day I saved some of my bread and carried it home to him. But if I had stayed, we would not have survived. I had to go but I think of him all the time."

It was equally as hard to leave brothers and sisters behind as it was to leave parents. It was her brother's unselfishness that prompted one girl to leave. She described how she had changed her mind about joining an orphanage when her brother, who was too old to be accepted, cried as she was preparing to leave. But her brother insisted that she go. He said it would make him happy to know that at least one member of the family had a chance to get out of Russia.

Some children thought about helping their families until the last minute. "Just before we were about to leave, my brother and I were each given a sweater by the orphanage," a boy recalled. "My brother ran home to give them to our brothers and sisters. Maybe they could trade them for bread. On the way, two bigger boys who wanted to steal the sweaters attacked my brother.

They beat him up, but he wouldn't let go of the sweaters. He knew it was the last help he could offer our family."

Lonek was struck by the children's resourcefulness in finding ways to overcome obstacles. One sixteen-year-old boy told how he had pretended to be only twelve years old because the orphanage wouldn't take older children. He had no problem passing himself off as a twelve-year-old because starvation had stunted his growth. But such tricks did not work for everyone. A girl said her seventeen-year-old sister tried to do the same but was recognized and taken off the train. Lonek began to wonder if his mother had been right in taking him to an orphanage. What had seemed like the end of the world to him was for many children the hope of a new beginning.

Some Jewish children talked about an added problem they encountered—anti-Semitism. Some orphanages refused to take in any Jewish children. In others, prejudiced directors gave more food to the Christian children than to the Jewish children. And some counselors looked away when Christian children ganged up on Jewish children and called them names or beat them up. As a result, some Jewish children pretended to be Christian in order to have an equal chance. One little girl described how her desperately sick father placed a cross around her neck so that the orphanage near them would accept her. Some time later, her father smuggled a note to her into the orphanage, asking her to always remember that she was Jewish.

The Jewish children's problem did not end even when they were admitted to an orphanage. Some prejudiced counselors prevented them from leaving Russia with General Anders' army.

General Anders was only allowed to take 30,000 civilians with him. These counselors wanted all the places to go to the Christian children. Lonek thought this was very unfair.

One boy said, "In my orphanage three transports had already left to join General Anders, but not a single Jewish child was allowed on any of them. The next transport had 320 Christian children, but only twenty of us Jewish children were allowed to go with them. I had to leave without my sister because they would not allow her to go with me."

Lonek was pleased to hear some children talk about Christian counselors who helped the Jewish children. A Jewish girl reported, "When we got to the train station, some soldiers would not allow any of the Jewish children onto the train. Luckily, when our counselor saw that the train was about to leave, she quickly pushed all of us onto the train. We lost all our belongings but they couldn't toss us off the train."

"Yes," another girl agreed, "A priest heard some Jewish children crying because they weren't allowed on the train. He ran up and down the station, and actually stopped the train from leaving until they were all on board."

An additional difficulty threatening the children was the ever-present NKVD. They watched the orphanages like vultures and followed the children until their departure. A teenage girl told her story in a voice that was almost a whisper, as if she were afraid that the Russian secret police could still be watching her.

"There were quite a few older children, ages fourteen to sixteen years old. The secret police was always hanging around our orphanage. We didn't even dare go outside into our courtyard.

Our director kept us older children hidden in the basement. When the NKVD came, she only took them to where the younger ones were and said, 'Let me show you our children. You can see they are playing. We cater only to little ones.' She was very brave. If the NKVD had discovered us, she would have been sent to a gulag with us. The orphanage didn't even have the proper documents for us to leave. Our director ran to the officials in charge and pleaded with them to let her have the necessary documents. We worked all through the night to get the papers filled out. We didn't sleep. In the morning, the director told us that the papers were all in order and we could leave. We jumped and danced for joy." Lonek listened to the children's stories. He thought about how much they had all endured to get on this train.

The counselors came to tell the children that they were heading for Persia [now Iran]. Lonek knew nothing about Persia, but that did not really matter. All he knew was that once he was in Persia, he would be beyond the reach of the Russians and Germans from whom he had been fleeing for so many months. There would be no Hitler, no Stalin, no NKVD, and no gulag.

*Three boys led out of Russia by General Anders' Army.*

# 16
# Goodbye Russia

When the children arrived at the Russian port of Krasnovodsk, there was no ship waiting to take them across the Caspian Sea to Persia. No provisions had been made for them at all; there were no tents, no blankets, and no food. And worse, there was hardly any clean drinking water, only some smelly liquid that tasted of gasoline.

Lonek found the wait for the boat very difficult. He often felt hungry and exhausted. He was very aware that he was still on Russian soil, especially when he saw some NKVD men. He guessed that they were looking for children over sixteen years old. Lonek knew that if they found any, they would most likely arrest them.

The children from Lonek's orphanage were not the only group waiting to leave. Children from other orphanages were already in Krasnovodsk when his group arrived, and more trucks filled with children kept arriving. The counselors had lists of the children's names, ages, and birthplaces. Some children did not know how old they were, or where they had been born. To some of the names, extra notes had been added, such as: "all trace of father lost after escape to south Russia"; "mother died in Poland,

*A soldier in General Anders' army.*

*Polish orphan.*

father in Russia"; "no recollection of any family members"; and "parents died in Russia, found by soldiers."

Also waiting at the port were Polish soldiers who were going to join Anders' Army. These men didn't have the crisp, military appearance Lonek associated with soldiers. Their uniforms were old and ragged. Some didn't even have boots. They seemed to be as hungry as the children were. In spite of his promise to outfit and provide food for General Anders' army, Stalin had provided barely enough food to keep them alive.

Everyone waited impatiently as one night passed, then a day, then another night. The children looked pale and had a haunted expression in their eyes. They were painfully thin and suffered from all kinds of ailments such as boils, ringworm, and stomach trouble. They waited in long lines when there was food, feeling faint and hoping for a little soup or a crust of bread. To Lonek they didn't look like children, but like soldiers returned from battle. Some children never let go of each other's hands. They wanted to make sure that during their final minutes in Russia they would not lose the last person they loved.

At last the ship to take them to Persia arrived, but the conditions on board were not much better than they had been at the port. There had been no time or money to stock the ship with adequate supplies. The captain had only one thing in mind: to squeeze as many Polish passengers as possible onto the ship and to get them out of Russia quickly. No one trusted Stalin to keep his promise to let General Anders and his followers leave. The number of passengers on the ship far exceeded the availability of space or the food. The atmosphere was full of tension.

As the ship pulled up anchor, Lonek had mixed feelings. On the one hand, he was thrilled to leave Russia. On the other hand, every mile took him further away from his family. Soon he would be in a foreign land, removed, possibly forever, from them.

Lonek felt as sad as he had when his mother left him at the orphanage door. He wandered around the deck by himself, tears streaming down his face. He found a little wooden barrel and sat down on it. He was overwhelmed by a longing for his mother, his father, and Heimek. Would he ever see them again? A few children tried to talk to him, but he didn't respond. A grown-up brought him some food, but he refused it. He was too sad to eat.

The crossing lasted twenty-four hours. The children slept on deck and ate whatever food was available. When the ship docked in Pahlevi, the harbor on the Persian side of the Caspian

Sea, a giant wave of relief swept over the passengers. As soon as they stepped on land they hugged and congratulated each other. It was wonderful to be out of Russia.

The Persian port was an improvement over the Russian port. There was still a food shortage and very few medical supplies for the many sick children. But here, at least, the children had tents to sleep in.

The biggest change was how the children felt—suddenly, they no longer felt terror. Lonek noticed a change within himself. The constant sense of dread that hung over him since the Germans invaded Poland had begun to lift. He started to feel lighthearted, free, and even happy.

After about three weeks the trucks that were to take the children to Teheran, the capital of Persia, finally arrived. The children were no longer going to the same destination as the soldiers. As the children were loaded into the trucks, the counselors wanted to place the very young and the sick children into separate trucks so they could receive special care. But the children refused to be separated from their brothers and sisters. Even though they were out of Russia, the children still feared that any separation might be final. They protested so loudly that the counselors let them climb aboard whichever truck they wanted.

The road to Teheran was lined with palm trees. During the day the tents the children slept in were loaded onto the roof of the trucks. When they stopped to camp for the night the counselors set up the tents while the children bathed and played in the sea. Friendly local people saw how thin and pale the children looked and brought them eggs, cocoa, fruit, and fresh water.

One of the older girls was thrilled when she was given a gift of some grapes. When a counselor called her away for a minute, she carefully counted each one before leaving them on her seat. While she was gone, Lonek watched a little girl come and inspect the grapes. It was obvious to him that she had never seen grapes before, and she couldn't resist trying one. Lonek laughed when she screwed up her little face in reaction to the sour taste. She did not take another. When the older girl returned and noticed that one of her precious grapes was missing, she started to pursue the little one with fury. Lonek stepped in to protect the little girl. From then on, Lonek was her hero. Lonek was coming out of his shell.

Lonek became very fond of the counselors. They were all young men who had been in the Polish army. They had volunteered to look after the children and were very devoted to them. They did whatever they could to comfort them. When any of the children felt sad, one of the counselors would always notice and gently try to comfort them. Their kindness made all the difference to the children.

Best of all, Lonek made new friends. Except for the Muslim boy in Tashkent, he had not had a friend since he left Jaroslaw. In fact, he not only found a friend, he found a little family. The family included a boy named Krauss. He was the same age as Lonek. He had an older sister, a red-haired teenager with a long ponytail. Wherever Krauss' sister went, she carried their baby brother who reminded Lonek of Heimek. She was like a mother to her two brothers. Soon she began to act like a mother to Lonek, too. She found special treats for them to eat and generally looked after their welfare. Lonek loved Krauss, his brother, and his sister, and spent most of his time with them. They were like a little family.

To reach the children's tent village, the trucks had to pass through Teheran. Lonek had never seen such a magnificent city before. It seemed huge and exciting to him with its big build-

*Lonek and Krauss.*

ings, beautiful homes, and lively streets. Lonek marveled at the shop windows filled with food and luxury items. Teheran was heaven. Lonek realized with relief that there were still places left in the world where fear did not lurk around every corner. He wondered what life in Teheran would bring.

# 17
# Teheran

The orphans were a ragged lot when they climbed off their trucks and entered the camp. They had started the journey in want of everything. But by now, after traveling by train, ship, and truck with barely any food or medicines, they looked half-dead. They looked sickly and feverish, and their skin was covered with rashes. Their eyes and cheeks were sunken and their heads had been shaved to get rid of lice. Their clothes were torn and thin and provided little protection against the evening cold. Most of the children didn't have shoes.

The camp in Teheran consisted of rickety tents that were full of holes. Each child was given a cotton pillow, three thin blankets, and a thin mattress. There were no chairs or tables. The children ate sitting on the ground. As usual, food was in short supply and the diet was very monotonous. Breakfast was bread, a dab of butter and jam, and an apple. Lunch was a little bowl of soup and more bread. Dinner was tea and an egg. Once in a while there were some dates, which Lonek considered a great treat.

Even though life in camp was an improvement, the children continued to be deeply affected by their past ordeal. Like Lonek, practically all of them had lost or been separated from their fam-

*Polish children upon arrival in Persia.*

ilies. Their distress showed itself in different ways. Some of the children continued to live in constant fear that something terrible was about to happen. They could not believe that they were safe now. Because of their terrible encounters with German and Russian soldiers, the NKVD, and Russian guards, some children had lost trust in all adults.

Added to the children's insecurities was their constant worry that there would not be any food the following day. They wore little hand-sewn bags that they hung around their necks, in which they placed any leftover food for the following day. Even after the food spoiled, the children would not let go of their insurance against hunger.

Because of the many worries, some children became depressed or angry with their fate. They found it difficult to put their feelings into words. Instead, they showed their distress through their behavior. Some became quiet and withdrawn; others cried often. Some got angry for no apparent reason and fought with other children. Some children clung to their counselors; others avoided all contact with them.

Another major problem was the continuing anti-Semitism

directed at the Jewish children by some of the Christian children and counselors. The Jewish children were constantly being teased, bullied, and deprived of their share of clothes and food. It weighed heavily upon them and made them fearful.

A young Jewish Polish ex-soldier by the name of David Laor was appointed head counselor in charge of the almost 1,000 Jewish children. Though he had little experience, he had great understanding of the children because he had suffered losses similar to theirs. He realized that his most important job was to make the children feel secure. He began by creating a separate camp for the Jewish children, which he would run together with other Jewish counselors. He called the camp "The Teheran Home for Jewish Children." Once in their own camp, the Jewish children would no longer be plagued by anti-Semitism.

In addition, David Laor created a comfortable routine for the children. Every morning Lonek and the other children got up, ate breakfast, and helped to tidy up their tents. Then they assembled around the flagpole in the center of camp. There they sang songs and raised their special flag which proudly proclaimed the camp's name. After the ceremony, the children attended classes. Lonek remembered how often he had complained about going to school when he lived in Jaroslaw. But ever since he stopped going to school, he really missed it. There were no textbooks, but the counselors designed the lessons so that books weren't necessary. Classes were taught in both Polish and Russian, which Lonek could now understand.

After classes, the children played sports and games. In addition, the children were encouraged to develop their own specific talents and to do something to contribute to life in the camp. Those who were skilled with a needle and thread made or mended clothes. Artistic children wrote poems or designed posters to decorate the camp. Lonek was good at making and fixing things, so whenever something in the camp broke, he volunteered to fix it. Lonek acquired a reputation for being inventive and able to solve mechanical problems.

The counselors worked hard at making the children feel safe and happy. They took turns walking between the tents at night, listening for crying children who had had nightmares, and stopping to comfort them. They were patient and understanding in trying to help the children with their personal problems. When one girl refused to do her chores unless she was paid with food, a counselor did not scold her. Instead he explained the meaning of cooperation to her. He assured her that she was with friends now who would share with her whatever they had. The counselors tried to reassure one little girl who cried constantly. She

*Polish children in camp in Teheran.*

insisted that she had seen her father through the window when the train was pulling out of the station in Tashkent. Now that she knew her father was alive, how would she possibly ever find him again? A boy who had lost his brother on the way to Tashkent wanted to leave the camp and search for him. The counselors listened patiently and promised to help the children search for their relatives. Lonek and the other children became very fond of the counselors.

"They are not taking care of us for money," Lonek said to Krauss. "They are doing it for love."

The counselors informed Lonek and the other Jewish children that they would be staying in Teheran for awhile, but their final destination was Palestine [now Israel]. They explained to the children that Jews had lived in Palestine for thousands of years. Now, many Jews who were scattered around the world wanted to return to Palestine and build a homeland there. These Jews were called Zionists. The Zionists believed that if the Jews had a country of their own, it would be easier for them to defend themselves against any future danger, such as another Hitler. Lonek hoped that there would not be any anti-Semitism in Palestine.

The counselors told the children that as soon as they received permission from the Iraqi government to cross Iraq, they would leave for Palestine. Lonek was as impatient as the others to leave and start a new life. He believed that this would happen soon, and there was no reason to expect any sudden, unpleasant surprises.

But he was wrong.

# 18
# Darkness

No one could understand how it happened. Not the counselors, not the nurses, not the doctors. Suddenly Lonek went blind. One sunny afternoon, as Lonek and Krauss were playing together, the world darkened for Lonek.

"Krauss, why is it suddenly so dark?" Lonek called out.

"Lonek, what are you talking about? It's only lunch time," Krauss said.

"But Krauss, I can't see! I can't see anything!" Krauss ran over to Lonek and put his face close to Lonek's. When he realized Lonek really couldn't see him, Krauss began to shake him frantically by the shoulders, as if he could shake the darkness from Lonek's eyes. Horrified, Krauss took Lonek by the hand and guided him to the infirmary tent. The nurse looked at Lonek with a puzzled expression, and then gently told him to sit down. She held up four fingers in front of Lonek's eyes.

"Lonek, how many fingers do you see?" she asked.

"I don't see anything!" Lonek replied in a shaky voice. "All I see is black."

"Wait here," the nurse said. A few minutes later she came back with the camp doctor, who was equally puzzled. The doctor arranged for Lonek to be brought to a nearby hospital. As a car arrived to take him away, Lonek could hear Krauss crying.

"Don't worry, Lonek." Krauss called out as Lonek was helped into the car. "You'll be all right. I'll come and see you!"

Lonek was petrified. He was alone, going—he did not know where—with a driver who did not speak a word to him. In this sudden darkness, he was feeling a new kind of fear. It was different from the all other kinds of terror he had experienced since the day his father had left to fight the Germans. To Lonek, not being able to see felt like the worst thing that had ever happened to him. In the past, when Lonek faced a challenge, he was able to work out a way to make things a little better. For the first time, he felt completely helpless.

The car stopped, and Lonek was taken into a building. He heard Polish voices, and guessed that he was inside a hospital run by General Anders' army. The voices he heard didn't sound kind or friendly. Someone ordered him to undress, and then led him to a bed in his underwear. Then, nothing. For the rest of that day and night he was left alone. Other than bringing him food, the nurses did not trouble themselves about him.

When he woke up the next day, Lonek heard the voices of people around him but no one spoke to him. He assumed the people were doctors and nurses. At one point a bandage was placed around Lonek's head. The bandage felt tight and uncomfortable, and he couldn't open his eyes. With nothing to do but sit and wait, Lonek couldn't ward off the worries that ran through his head constantly. "Why can't I see? Will I ever be able to see again? And if I can't see, will I ever be allowed to go back to the Teheran Children's Home? What if everyone in the camp leaves for Palestine while I am in the hospital? Will everyone just forget about me, and leave? No," he tried to reassure himself, "Krauss will remind the counselors. He won't let them go without me."

From time to time, panic overcame Lonek as he started to think that he might be sent back to Russia. The thought was so terrible that he hid his head under his pillow, trying to shut out the pictures that rushed through his mind. But the troubling thoughts remained. He thought of his father, lying feverish and uncomplaining on a slab of wood for a bed. Was his father still sick? Was he worse? He remembered his mother wiping his father's burning forehead with a wet rag. He remembered the long walks he took with his mother in Jaroslaw. He imagined Heimek playfully trying to run between everyone's legs. Lonek suddenly began to worry about Heimek. What if he were alone right now, like himself? Heimek was so little; he wouldn't be able to take care of himself! No, he was probably with his mother. Lonek desperately wished his mother were with him now.

Lonek had never felt so lonely in his life. Hours passed without a single word said to him or by him. The first time his food was brought, it was just left on his bed by his legs, and he accidentally knocked it off the bed. From then on, when food was left for him, Lonek would carefully find the edges of the tray and place it on his lap. When he ran his fingers over the plate, they would stop in the soft food. He ate slowly so he wouldn't drop or spill any of it. Even though the food was tasteless and badly cooked, eating helped pass the time and he knew it made him stronger.

The other hospital patients were very unfriendly to Lonek. They called him names, and sometimes took away his tray of food. And when Lonek got out of bed, they put chairs and blankets in his way to make him trip. Lonek got angry and decided that he had to protect himself. He drew his few possession near to himself so that he could safeguard them. One afternoon Lonek did get out of bed, and by walking very slowly with his hands stretched out in front of him, managed to find his way outside. He found a bench, and sat down. He spent several hours just listening to the birds, and enjoying the feeling of the fresh air on his face. But his spirits didn't really lift until the day Krauss arrived for a visit. The two boys talked and laughed the whole time. The visit renewed Lonek's spirit, and helped him feel that all would be well again soon.

One week passed. Then two. Then three. Then four, five, and six. Lonek felt as if he had been in the hospital forever. Then suddenly the hoped for miracle happened. One morning, Lonek woke up and saw some light through the bandages. At first he thought he was still dreaming. He sat up in bed and blinked his eyes over and over. But it was not just a dream. Lonek was really able to tell day from night. He was beside himself with joy. Almost daily, the light got brighter. After some time, Lonek noticed that while the doctor changed his bandages he was able to see shadowy figures. To his immense relief, the doctor told him that he would regain his sight completely.

Several days later, the doctor replaced Lonek's huge bandage with a smaller one. It had little slits in it. Lonek felt as if he had been reborn. Every now and then he cheated a little and enlarged the slits with his fingers. As Lonek saw more, he became happier and happier.

When Lonek's sight was almost fully recovered, a counselor came to take him back to the camp, and explained that Lonek's blindness had been caused by his years of starvation and malnutrition. Now, the camp's kitchen would make sure that he received all of the vitamins he needed.

When Lonek returned to camp, the children received him warmly. But he received the most enthusiastic reception from Krauss and the rest of his family. Lonek was struck by how much the children had changed while was away. They seemed happier and more cooperative. Classes were held regularly, and in the afternoon the children had gymnastics and played soccer. Lonek played with Krauss every day, and spent much time with the rest of his little family.

There was only one major problem left. The Iraqi officials refused to allow the Jewish orphans and their counselors to cross Iraq. At that time, the Iraqis did not want to help any more Jews to enter Palestine, but it was the shortest and most direct way. Lonek wondered whether they would have to stay in Persia forever.

Every day there were rumors. "We're leaving next week." "We aren't going." "Tomorrow permission to cross will come from Iraq." "The Iraqis have denied permission." Everybody including the counselors were becoming impatient. It seemed that they would never get permission to cross Iraq. Almost 1,000 children were stuck in Persia. Lonek became increasingly discouraged. What he did not know was that help was on its way.

# 19
# The Final Exit

The orphans had arrived in Teheran at the beginning of summer, 1942. At first, Lonek had been told that they would leave for Palestine at the end of summer. Then he was told it would be fall. Then winter came. Surely, he thought, they would leave by New Year's. When New Year's came, he and Krauss sat sadly on their mattresses in their tent and tried to console each other.

"Lonek, do you think we will ever get to Palestine?" Krauss asked. "I'm starting to believe we'll never go."

"No, Krauss, we will. You saw the maps. David showed us where we are going. He wrote out the whole journey. He wouldn't do that if he didn't think we are going."

Though Lonek and Krauss did not know it, the governments of England and America were determined to help the children. They had been trying to persuade the Iraqis to allow the children to cross their country in order to reach Palestine. Finally it became clear that the Iraqis would never agree. Another way to transport the children would have to be found.

At first they considered flying the children over Iraq to Palestine. Many planes would be needed, but none could be spared because they were being used to fly troops to battle zones.

There was only one other solution: send the children by sea to Palestine. It would be a long and perilous journey. The children would have to travel by a very dangerous route which led through the Persian Gulf, the Gulf of Oman, and the Red Sea. Most of the children had never even heard of these faraway places. The final lap of the journey would be by train to Palestine. Although it was almost as difficult to find a ship as a plane, the dedicated government officials finally located one.

On January 6, 1943, just when the children's and the counselors' spirits were sinking, a counselor came running into the tent where classes were being held and announced excitedly, "Everybody, listen! We have just been informed that we are

*Children preparing for departure from Teheran.*

leaving. Get ready! Pack your things." There wasn't much to pack. Lonek took his few possessions and his little bag for left-over food, and he was ready to leave.

Lonek had thought that he couldn't wait for this moment to arrive. To his surprise, he suddenly felt scared. He was used to the camp, to the routine, to his tent mates, and to the counselors. He liked having the same faces around him day after day. He looked forward to the daily soccer games. Now he was struck by the realization that things would change once he left the camp. He feared that what would come might be worse than the present. The many disappointing twists of fate Lonek had experienced made him distrustful of change. He was not alone in this fear. He noticed that many of the other children felt the same way. As the orphans prepared to leave the camp, some of them cried, and the younger children clung to the older ones.

On the day of departure, the children boarded a long line of old, beaten-up trucks bound for the port of Bandar-e-Shahpur at the head of the Persian Gulf. There, a ship was waiting for them. The drivers covered the open trucks to prevent the children from seeing the narrow, curvy, unpaved, mountainous road on which they were traveling. The trucks were so rickety that an equal number of children had to sit on each side of the truck to balance out the weight. Otherwise the truck might turn over and fall down the steep cliffs. Each time the truck traveled around a sharp curve, the driver made the children get off the truck and walk. Even the driver was afraid of toppling off the road.

After thirty-six hours, the groggy, sleep-deprived children arrived at the harbor. A ship called the *Dunera* was waiting there. It was called a ship, but to Lonek it looked more like a huge, old, iron tub. Once he was on board, Lonek looked around, and what he saw was not inviting. There were no tables, chairs or beds. There were hammocks, but not nearly enough for 1,000 children. Lonek decided he would rather sleep on the deck of the ship, anyway.

The ship was poorly prepared in other ways, too. There was a shortage of fresh water, so the children had to wash themselves and their clothes in seawater. And almost everyone became seasick. The children were constantly throwing up on themselves and each other. But Lonek did not let the grimy conditions of the ship upset him. He was too close to his destination. There was only one thing that disturbed Lonek. Except for David Laor, he did not see any of the usual counselors on board the *Dunera*. They were all gone and a new group of counselors had taken their place. Lonek asked David what had happened to the counselors that had been with the children all along. David Laor always answered the children's questions in an honest and straightforward way, but this time he evaded the question. It puzzled Lonek that David did not seem to know. For Lonek and Krauss, the disappearance of the counselors was just one more example that life was unpredictable.

The ship's captain was very concerned about the safety of the children. He was afraid that German fighter planes might attack the ship, so he insisted that the children stay below deck much of the time, where they would be safer. But Lonek knew that if the ship were bombed or hit a mine, it would be almost impossible for them to escape from the depths of the ship.

Every morning, Lonek hoped that by evening they would reach their destination, but the ship kept sailing on. It was two weeks before the captain announced that their first stop was in view.

The ship anchored in Karachi, a port city in India [now in Pakistan]. Lonek was shocked by what he saw there. Men dressed in dirty rags, who were so thin that they looked like skeletons, climbed over the side of the ship and ran to a corner of the deck where the kitchen staff had thrown away the leftover food. Though it was spoiled and smelled bad, the starving men began to fight over the garbage. Lonek had never seen such wretchedness outside of the gulag.

As Lonek traveled by truck through Karachi, he was stunned by the difference between the rich and poor people. In the busy markets, elegant men wearing turbans and lovely ladies dressed in beautiful silk saris contrasted with handi-capped beggars and starving people.

Lonek and the other children passed snake charmers playing music that coaxed snakes to rise up out of their baskets. He laughed at a dressed-up monkey sitting on a man's shoulder and at a group of little monkeys who held hands and performed tricks. He was surprised that cows wandered freely through the streets. Lonek asked one of the counselors about this. He explained that most people here were Hindus, and that they believed cows were sacred.

The combination of the fairy-tale setting, the strange customs, and the stark poverty of Karachi fascinated Lonek. He felt cheerful and upbeat when he arrived at the Karachi camp,

*Children wearing the new clothes and pith helmets they received in Karachi.*

which was located in a beautiful meadow. Carefully laid out pathways led to small, comfortable tents, four children per tent. Each child had a cot with sheets and mosquito netting to prevent the malaria-carrying mosquitoes from biting them at night.

When members of India's Jewish population had heard that a ship full of orphans was arriving, they donated money and supplies to the camp. The children were given pith helmets to protect their heads from the burning sun. They were also each given a pair of shorts, white shirts, and a new pair of shoes. Lonek had not felt so clean and fresh in a long time.

Indian soldiers stood guard over their camp at night. Lonek tried to talk to them, but they just looked at him blankly. He tried Hebrew, Polish, Russian, and Yiddish, but the guards had never heard such languages spoken. Lonek could not understand any of the languages the guards spoke. The guards' impressive-looking turbans fascinated him. The only scary thing was the howling of hyenas at night. Throughout the night, campfires were kept burning to keep the wild animals away.

David Laor tried to keep to the same routine in Teheran as the children had had in the camp. In the morning, they marched to the flagpole where they sang songs. Now a different flag flew in the center of the camp. It was the white and blue Jewish flag. Classes were held outdoors or in a tent. In the afternoons the children played sports. Lonek was told that they would not stay long in this camp. They were waiting for a ship that would take them through the Gulf of Oman and the Red Sea to Port Said in Egypt. There they would board a train for Palestine.

On February 6th, about two weeks after the children arrived in Karachi, Lonek and the other children boarded the *SS Noralea*. To Lonek it didn't look much better than the *Dunera* and the journey was just as dangerous. Everyone knew that the sea was full of mines and German submarines.

The captain wanted to avoid the floating mines so he sent a few small boats ahead of the ship to look out for them. The ship moved very slowly, with sailors posted around the clock to look out for any signs of danger. Whenever they spotted a suspicious-looking object, they sounded an alarm. The sound frightened the children, who never knew whether it was safer to be below or above on deck. One day, Lonek felt the ship give a big shudder. A torpedo had just missed the ship, but the impact of its explosion sent an enormous vibration through the water. Lonek trembled almost as much as the ship.

The *SS Noralea* made a brief stop in Yemen, an Islamic country with strict rules about how females are allowed to dress and behave. While the ship was in the port, all the girls had to go below deck, where it was stiflingly hot. The captain explained that their short skirts and sleeveless dresses would offend the local people.

*A troop ship, the type Lonek traveled on.*

Excitement mounted when the ship finally entered the Red Sea on its journey north. Lonek had heard the Biblical story of Moses, and how the waters of the Red Sea parted to allow the Jews to flee from the pursuing Egyptians. He thought about his own journey, and how the Red Sea was serving to help him escape from the Russians.

Finally, on February 17th, the ship dropped anchor at Port Said, Egypt. Lonek and Krauss became more and more elated, and more and more impatient. They were now only a short train ride away from Palestine.

The water in Port Said was too shallow for the SS *Noralea* to pull in and dock at the pier. The children had to climb down ladders into small boats and be rowed ashore. As Lonek and Krauss looked over the railing, waiting for the little boats to arrive to take them to shore, they saw something that suddenly gripped them with fear. Soldiers were lined up along the side of the long pier. Lonek and Krauss held on to each other, fearing that Russian soldiers had finally caught up with them, but then they noticed that the soldiers were actually smiling at them. The soldiers were calling to them and throwing them little packages. Lonek caught one and unwrapped it; it was filled with many different kinds of sweets. These soldiers were certainly unlike any he had ever seen. The counselors explained that the soldiers were members of the Jewish Brigade, which was serving with the British Army. They had come for the sole purpose of welcoming the children. The passengers were rowed to shore by boat. The first to go were the caretakers carrying babies. The next to disembark were the younger children. Finally, Lonek and Krauss and the older children followed them. As they descended into the little boats, the counselors led them in a song they had learned, "We sing and rise above death and ruin."

Everyone was filled with joy. The captain was delighted that he had delivered the children safely. The counselors were happy to have helped the children through their journey. And the children were thrilled that at last they were only one short train ride away from Palestine. One of the soldiers put his hand on Lonek's shoulder and said, "With so many children lost during the war, it's a miracle that you are here. We welcome you."

The next morning, carrying little blue-and-white Jewish flags, the children sang *Hatikva*, the Jewish national song. Then they climbed aboard the train bound for Palestine, the final stop in their amazing journey.

# 20
# Welcome Home

The train was packed—there wasn't one empty seat. Having no place else to sit, Lonek and Krauss climbed into the luggage rack above the seats. The boys watched the passing scenery with delight and gloried in the happiness of the moment. They marveled at the green trees ripe with fruit that had turned the desert into a paradise.

As the train slowed to its first stop in Palestine, Lonek and Krauss jumped off their perch. They joined the children who were crowding around the windows. To their astonishment, they saw a station platform filled with hundreds of people who were waving, crying, and cheering. At first, Lonek didn't grasp what the people were so excited about. Then suddenly he realized they were there to welcome the children! He thought that every Jewish man, woman, and child living in Palestine must have left home just to welcome the orphans. Lonek and the other children happily waved back.

When the children disembarked, smiling women pushed to the front and kissed and hugged the children as if they were their own. A sobbing woman embraced Lonek. "It's a miracle! It's a wonder!" she exclaimed. "A thousand children saved! We have lost so many, and now you are here! You really are here!"

*The orphans arrive in Palestine to the excited welcome of the local people.*

Lonek realized that these joyous women had come to welcome, soothe, and celebrate the arrival of the children. They brought chocolate, cookies, and little gifts. They knew that these children had lost so much, and they wanted to make them smile.

Despite the jubilation and excitement of the moment, there was also an undercurrent of sadness. Almost everyone at the station had lost at least one family member. Many had come with the hope of finding a familiar face. Some had hoped against hope that perhaps their child, their sister, their brother, their nephew, or niece might be on that train. Or maybe one of the children had news of someone they loved. "What is your name?" they asked. "What town in Poland do you come from?" "Did you ever hear of my daughter (or 'my son,' or 'my friend's child')?"

Occasionally cries of joy rang out from the crowd. One boy

from the train found his brother, the only other survivor of his family. A girl found a former school friend on the platform. A woman ran to a boy just getting off the train and explained to him that she was his aunt. He didn't remember her because he had been too young when he last saw her in Poland, but he was thrilled to find he still had a relative.

*This boy does not recognize his aunt who has come to pick him up from the train.*

*The children were lined up soon after their arrival in Palestine.*

Lonek and Krauss were overwhelmed. Only a year before they had been prisoners and outcasts. Suddenly they were special. People actually wanted to know their names, give them gifts, and make them happy.

"See, to them we are a miracle," Lonek said to Krauss. "We survived. Just picture a house that burned down to the ground and the owner finds some precious family jewels in the ashes. That's us."

That evening, the exhausted children were taken to a camp that had been lovingly made ready for them. A big sign saying "Welcome Home" was prominently displayed. There were beds with spotless white sheets, warm new blankets, and soft pillows. Smiling women brought them glasses of fresh milk. Hot showers were available, and all the children were given new clothes. Local children presented them with the bread and salt that by custom is given to welcome strangers. There was a special dinner to welcome the children. The table was loaded with more delicious-looking food than Lonek had ever seen. The main attractions were two mountains of oranges. The children stuffed them in their pockets, convinced that such an opportunity would never come again.

When Lonek went to bed that night, he couldn't fall asleep. His mind was full of memories of his journey. It was almost impossible to count the many lucky circumstances that had made it possible for him to survive. What if the German officer in Jaroslaw had shot his father? What if the farmer whom his father had sent to fetch them had betrayed them to the Germans? What if Sosa's father had not been willing to hide them? What if his father and mother had been too weak to survive the cattle-car rides, the harsh work and the freezing winter in Siberia? What if Lonek's father had not been so resourceful and always found them shelter? What if he, Lonek, had not been able to help his family find additional food? What if Stalin, who killed thousands of Poles, hadn't given permission for the Polish prisoners to leave the gulag? What if the ships Lonek sailed on had been bombed or hit by a mine or a torpedo? Lonek could hardly believe how many dangers he had managed to survive.

Lonek would never forget these events. But from that moment on, he would not have to deal with desperate hunger, fear, calamity, and loneliness. He would no longer have to be preoccupied with the struggle to survive. In the warmth and safety of his surroundings, there was only one thing missing—his family. "Maybe my family has survived. Maybe I will see them again," he thought. And he remembered his father's words, "We must never give up hope." He knew his father was right. With that thought, Lonek fell asleep contentedly.

Lonek had left his home in September 1939, when he was eleven years old. He had been on his journey for more than three years. He had traveled 12,150 miles.

Now, finally, he was home.

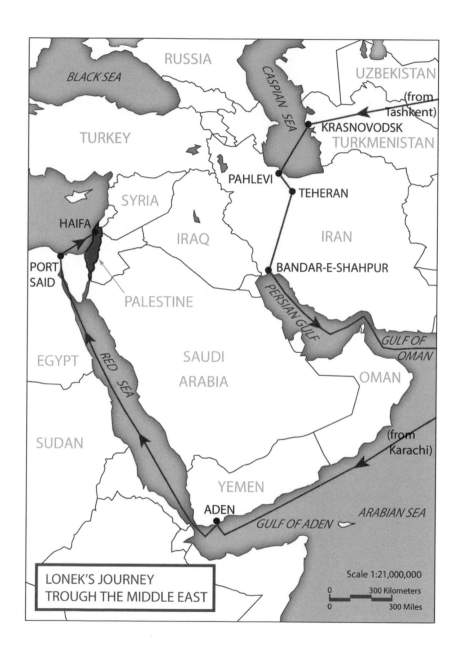

BLACK SEA

RUSSIA

UZBEKISTAN

(from Tashkent)

CASPIAN SEA

KRASNOVODSK

TURKEY

TURKMENISTAN

PAHLEVI

TEHERAN

SYRIA

IRAN

HAIFA

IRAQ

BANDAR-E-SHAHPUR

PORT SAID

PALESTINE

PERSIAN GULF

GULF OF OMAN

EGYPT

RED SEA

SAUDI

ARABIA

OMAN

SUDAN

(from Karachi)

YEMEN

ARABIAN SEA

ADEN

GULF OF ADEN

LONEK'S JOURNEY
TROUGH THE MIDDLE EAST

Scale 1:21,000,000

0   300 Kilometers

0   300 Miles

*Lonek in Palestine.*

# Afterword

Since this is a true story, you might like to know what happened to Lonek after he arrived in Palestine.

**With whom did Lonek live when he came to Palestine?**
Each child was given the choice of being placed with a family, living in a boarding school, or becoming a member of a kibbutz, a communal farm. Lonek told his counselor that living in a kibbutz would remind him too much of living in the gulag. Even though his counselor explained that a kibbutz is a happy place, Lonek could not be persuaded. Lonek did not want to live with a strange family either. He wanted to live with other children. So Lonek chose a boarding school.

**How did Lonek do in school?**
Since Lonek had missed more than three years of school, teachers helped him to make up the missed work. He did well in school, and caught up fairly quickly. The principal of the school was so impressed with Lonek's gift for fixing things that he urged him to transfer to a school that specialized in engineering and mechanics. Lonek wanted to do that, but he didn't have enough money to pay for the entrance exam, let alone for tuition. The principal helped raise money for Lonek to take the exam. Because Lonek did well on it, he won a scholarship to the engineering school.

**What did Lonek do after he finished high school?**

By the time Lonek finished high school, Palestine had become the country we now know as Israel. Because Israel was at war, Lonek joined the army. The Israeli army had very few tanks and very little money to buy any. Lonek's job was to build tanks from used parts that the government obtained. When tanks were partly destroyed in battle, Lonek rebuilt them. He played a major role in rebuilding three tanks in the middle of a battle, risking his life in the process.

**What had happened to his family?**

Some time after Lonek left Tashkent, his father recovered from his illness. Eventually he found a job that paid very little, but the family, once again, had some income. When the war in Europe finally ended, Lonek's parents and brother wanted to go to Israel to find Lonek. But Stalin would not allow anyone to leave Russia. As a result, Lonek's family tried to leave secretly. They attempted to cross the border out of Russia at night. But a Russian border guard caught them, and they were imprisoned for several months. When they were released, they again tried to cross the border. Again, they were caught and imprisoned, this time for an even longer period. Still, they didn't give up. When they were released for the second time, they tried again to escape and were caught again. But this time, they were caught by a Russian officer who sympathized with the family. Instead of arresting Lonek's parents, the officer helped them cross the border. Finally, they made it out of Russia.

### Was Lonek reunited with his family?

Lonek never stopped hoping that someday he would find his family. He discovered that he had an older cousin who had reached Palestine before him. His cousin often visited him at his boarding school, and Lonek was happy to find a family member nearby.

While Lonek was in the army, he learned that his parents and Heimek were alive. The division of the Red Cross that helps families separated during war to find each other, located Lonek's family in Germany, where they had gone after leaving Russia. They were trying to get to Israel from Germany to join Lonek.

One day, Lonek's superior officer called him into his office, and told Lonek that his parents and brother had arrived in Israel. By then, they had been separated for ten years. At first, Lonek and his family hardly recognized one another. Lonek's parents were very weak and sickly. Lonek took good care of them and nursed them back to health. In time, Lonek's parents and brother learned to speak Hebrew, the language of Israel.

After some time, Lonek's father was well enough to get a job. Lonek's mother again took care of the family. Lonek had longed for his mother's cooking when the family was imprisoned. Now he enjoyed her cooking once again. Heimek went to school in Israel and continued to live there.

**What did Lonek do in later years?**

Lonek worked as an engineer and inventor. He invented machinery needed by different industries. Lonek married and moved to the United States because his wife's parents lived there. They had two children—a boy and a girl. Lonek was immensely proud when he become a United States citizen.

**Did Lonek ever go back to visit Poland or Russia?**

Lonek never went back to Russia. But he did take Heimek on a visit to Jaroslaw and Lvov. Heimek had been too young when they lived in those cities to remember either place. But Lonek remembered all the familiar houses and streets in Jaroslaw. In Lvov, he showed Heimek the big, beautiful building where they had slept sixty people to a room. He also took him to the same bakery where he had waited in line for hours to buy a small piece of bread. When Lonek and Heimek revisited the store as adults, they bought some bread and ate it happily, right there in front of the store.

**What happened to Sosa?**

Lonek never knew for sure what happened to Sosa. When Lonek went back to Poland he learned that when the German Army invaded Russia there had been heavy fighting in the area of Sosa's village. The village had been totally destroyed and never rebuilt. Lonek hoped that Sosa's father, who was very resourceful and practical, had been able to flee with his family before the Nazis arrived.

**What happened to Krauss?**

While Lonek was in the army, he lost touch with Krauss. Lonek looked his name up in the telephone directories of any town he passed through in Israel and even in the United States. Lonek was never able to find him. Lonek didn't know if Krauss had moved to a different country, or what had happened to him. Lonek always considered Krauss one of the best friends he ever had, and was sure that Krauss felt the same about him.

**What happened to the counselors who suddenly disappeared during the voyage from Teheran?**

The counselors did not want to be absorbed into General Anders' army. They wanted to fight as part of the Jewish Brigade in the British army. In order to do so, they had to reach Palestine immediately. In order to be able to cross Iraq without that country's permission, they disguised themselves as Arabs. But since they did not speak the local language, they pretended to be deaf and unable to speak, in case anyone tried to question them. In this way, they secretly made their way through Iraq to Palestine. There they joined the Jewish Brigade of the British army and joined in the fight against Nazi Germany.

**What happened to the non-Jewish children who were freed from the gulags?**

The adults and children who were allowed to leave Russia with General Anders' Army went to refugee camps in many different countries. The children without families were sent to orphanages and foster homes in India, New Zealand, Mexico, South Africa, and other countries in Africa. After World War II, many Polish people did not want to go back to Poland, so they settled in countries around the world, and became proud citizens of their adopted countries.

**What happened to the Polish soldiers who joined General Anders Army?**

From Teheran, the soldiers went to Egypt where they were attached to the British army. They fought in Africa and Europe, and made a great contribution to the victory over Germany. The Polish pilots were based in Britain and became part of the British Royal Air force. They helped defend Britain against German air attacks. They also participated in the liberation of France. Wherever they fought, they were among the fiercest and most decorated soldiers.

**How did Lonek's memory of those difficult years affect him later in life?**

Although Lonek was happy as an adult, he never forgot the terrible things he experienced as a child. Whenever he thought of how he felt standing alone in the dark in front of the orphanage, his eyes welled up with tears. He treasured every moment of being with his family.

Lonek carried with him other scars from his past as well. He never fully recovered from the fear of going hungry. Whenever he went grocery shopping, he always bought more than one of each item on his list. He felt the need to reassure himself that he would have enough food for the next day, and the day after that.

Lonek never wasted even the smallest piece of bread. And he taught his children to treat food just as respectfully as he did. Remembering the times when he would have given anything for just one bite of bread, for the rest of his life Lonek regarded bread as more precious than gold.

# Glossary

**anti-Semite:** someone who dislikes Jews.

**Bandar-e-Shahpur:** now known as Bandar-e-Imam Khomeini, a port town at the head of the Persian Gulf in southwest Iran.

**Caspian Sea:** the largest lake in the world, located between Iran and Russia.

**cattle car:** a freight car that is used to transport cattle. During World War II, prisoners of the Soviet Union were deported to forced labor camps and were transported in cattle cars.

**commandant:** the commanding officer of a military organization.

**dysentery:** an inflammation of the lower intestine that is caused by a bacterial infection. The symptoms are pain, fever, diarrhea, and the passage of blood and mucous.

**gulag:** a forced labor camp or prison in the Soviet Union.

**Gulf of Oman:** an arm of the Arabian Sea just south of the Persian Gulf, connecting the Persian Gulf to the Arabian Sea.

**Hatikva:** the national anthem of Israel.

**Hitler, Adolf (1889-1945):** founder of the Nazi Party and chancellor of the Third Reich; ruled as an absolute dictator in Germany between 1933 and 1945. Hitler's regime is infamous for killing millions of people, particularly Jews, Poles, gypsies, and homosexuals. He committed suicide in 1945.

**Israel:** In 1948, the state of Israel was created as a Jewish state by a vote of the United Nations. It is in the Middle East bound by the Jordan River and the Mediterranean Sea.

**Jewish Brigade Group:** formed of fifteen Palestinian Jewish battalions that were incorporated into the British Army in 1940. The Jewish Brigade was made up of Jewish volunteers from Palestine.

**Karachi:** former capital of Pakistan, which separated from India in 1947 and became a separate country (current capital is Islamabad). Located on the Arabian Sea, Karachi is the largest city in Pakistan.

**kibbutz:** a collective settlement in Israel. On a kibbutz, chores are divided and assigned equally and children are raised communally.

**Krasnovodsk:** a port city on the Caspian Sea, now known as Turkmenbashi; located in western Turkmenistan.

**Lvov:** A city in west central Ukraine near the Polish border. The city belonged to Poland from 1918 until 1945, when it was surrendered to the Soviet Union at the end of World War II.

**malaria:** an often fatal infectious disease spread by the Anopheles mosquito. The symptoms are fever, chills, and profuse sweating.

**Nazi Party:** the German political party (National Socialist German Workers' party) that Adolf Hitler brought to power in 1933.

**NKVD:** the Soviet secret police.

**Pahlevi Harbor:** seaport in Iran, now known as Bandar-e Anzali; located on the Caspian Sea.

**Pakistan:** a Muslim country that was formerly a part of India and separated from India in 1947. Both India and Pakistan achieved independence from the United Kingdom in 1947.

**Palestine:** a region that is often referred to as the "Holy Land," historic Palestine has been occupied by Jews, Egyptians, Arabs, Romans, Byzantines, and Turks.

**pellagra:** a disease caused by starvation. The symptoms are a rash and nervous and digestive system problems.

**Persia:** an Islamic country in the Middle East that was known as Persia until 1935 and now is known as Iran.

**Persian Gulf:** an arm of the Arabian Sea just north of the Gulf of Oman and between western Iran and the Arabian peninsula.

**Port Said:** a city in northeast Egypt at the mouth of the Suez Canal, on the Mediterranean Sea.

**ration card:** a card that entitles a person to collect his/her share of rationed products.

**Red Cross:** an international organization, established by the Geneva Convention of 1864 at the urging of Jean Henri Dunant. It takes care of sick, wounded, and homeless people during wartime or following natural disasters.

**Red Sea:** an arm of the Indian Ocean that lies between northern Africa and the Arabian peninsula, and is connected to the Mediterranean Sea by the Suez Canal.

**refugee:** a person who is in danger of being persecuted because of political or religious beliefs and has fled his/her country in order to seek asylum in another country.

**scurvy:** a disease caused by a vitamin C deficiency. The symptoms are bleeding gums, bleeding under the skin, and extreme weakness.

**Siberia:** a region of northern central Russia that is 5.3 million square miles large and known for its desolation and extreme temperatures. During the Communist regime, people out of favor with the Soviet government were deported to slave camps in Siberia.

**SS:** the Nazi military unit that served to enforce Hitler's rule in Germany and the occupied countries. German abbreviation for Schutz Staffel, which literally means "protection staff."

**Stalin, Josef (1879-1953):** the despotic Russian dictator who succeeded Lenin as head of the Communist Party. He was responsible for the deaths of millions of Russians and other people.

**synagogue:** a building used by people of the Jewish faith for meeting, worship, and/or religious instruction.

**Tashkent:** the capital of present-day Uzbekistan. Tashkent was annexed by Russia in 1865; in 1930 it became the capital of the Uzbek Soviet Socialist Republic.

**Teheran:** the capital of Iran, located in the north; commonly known as Tehran.

**typhus:** an infectious disease transmitted by fleas, lice, and mites. The symptoms are high fever, headaches, delirium, and a rash.

**USSR:** The Union of Soviet Socialist Republics (Soviet Union). A union of 15 republics formed in 1922 as a Communist state and ended in 1991 when each republic became an independent country. Uzbekistan and Turkmenistan are two of the former soviet Republics.

**Uzbek:** 1) a Turkic inhabitant of Uzbekistan. 2) the Turkic language spoken by the Uzbeks.

**Wladislaw Anders:** the Polish general who commanded the allied Polish forces in the Middle East and Italy during World War II.

**Yemen:** a country founded in 1990 (when North Yemen and South Yemen joined to form the Republic of Yemen) in the southwest part of the Arabian Peninsula, on the Indian Ocean.

**Yiddish:** a German dialect that includes Hebrew words, is written in the Hebrew script, and is spoken by Jews throughout the world.

**Zionists:** supporters of a Jewish movement, founded by Theodor Herzl in 1897, that promoted the Jews' return to the land of Israel (Zion). Zionists were concerned with reestablishing a Jewish homeland in an effort to secure a safe haven for Jews from the anti-Semitism that was growing rampant throughout Europe.

# Photo Credits:

Cover:    Top: Same as p. 61
          Middle: Courtesy of Eliott Yaron
          Bottom: USHMM, courtesy of David Laor

Ends:     Map of Europe, Middle East, East Asia in 1942 by Jin Choi

P. 11:     Map of the Partition of Poland by Jin Choi

P. 12:     Photographed by M. Widerynski

P. 18:     USHMM, courtesy of Julien Bryan

P. 26:     Pilsudski Institute of America Archives

P. 35:     USHMM, courtesy of Instytut Pamieci Narodowej

P. 38:     Photographed by P. Krassowski

P. 46:     USHMM, courtesy of National Archives

P. 61:     Courtesy of the Tomek Wisniewski Collection (www.szukamypolski.com). This photo was sourced through the Kresy-Siberia Group (www.Kresy-Siberia.com), which is dedicated to researching, remembering, and recognizing the Polish citizens deported, enslaved, and killed by the Soviet Union during World War II.

P. 71:     Pilsudski Institute of America Archives

P. 75:     Pilsudski Institute of America Archives

P. 89:     Pilsudski Institute of America Archives

P. 98:     Pilsudski Institute of America Archives

P. 100:    Top: Pilsudski Institute of America
           Bottom: Pilsudski Institute of America

P. 104:    Courtesy of Eliott Yaron

P. 106:    Pilsudski Institute of America Archives

P. 108:    USHMM, courtesy of David Laor

P. 116:    USHMM, courtesy of David Laor

P. 120:    USHMM, courtesy of David Laor

P. 122:    Pilsudski Institute of America Archives

P. 125:    USHMM, courtesy of David Laor

P. 126:    Top: Central Zionist Archives
           Bottom: USHMM, courtesy of David Laor

P. 129:    Map of the Middle East by Jin Choi

P. 130:    Courtesy of Eliott Yaron

Map of Europe, the Middle East, and East Asia in 1942.